How to Set Boundaries
(Without Feeling Like a D*ck)

Jennifer A. Febel

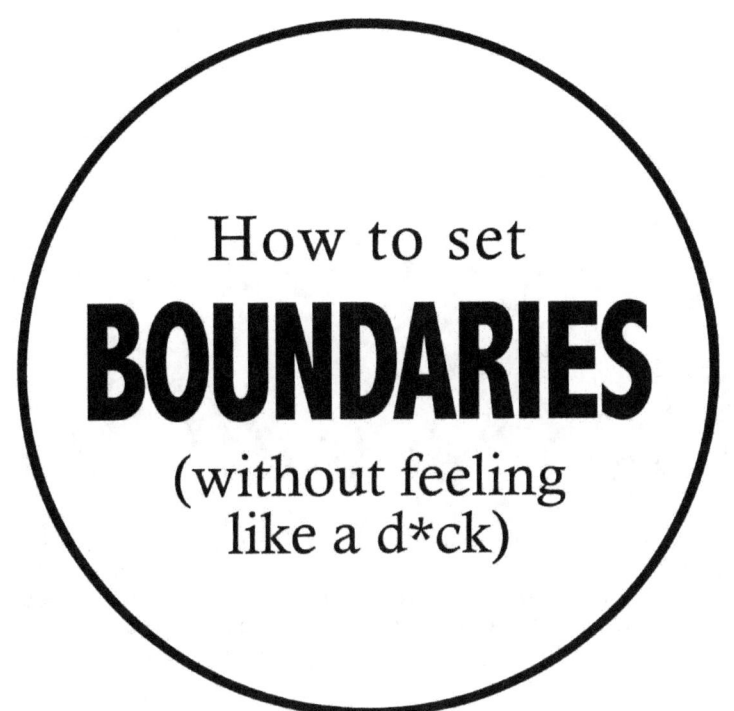

Jennifer A. Febel

Copyright © 2024 by Jennifer A. Febel

All Rights Reserved

ISBN: 978-1-7380814-0-0

Disclaimer: No part of this publication may be reproduced, distributed, or transmitted in any form or by any means, including photocopying, recording, or other electronic or mechanical methods, without the prior written permission of the author, except in the case of brief quotations embodied in reviews and certain other non-commercial uses permitted by copyright law.

All reasonable efforts have been made to ensure the accuracy and completeness of the information contained in this publication. However, the author and publisher assume no responsibility for errors or omissions and disclaim any liability for any loss or damage arising from the use or misuse of the information presented. This publication is intended to provide general information and is not a substitute for professional advice, including medical, psychiatric, or psychological consultation. Always seek the advice of a licensed healthcare provider with any health-related concerns.

Some names, locations, and identifying details have been changed to protect privacy.

Cover design by Jennifer A. Febel
Illustrations by Jennifer A. Febel
First Edition, 2024

This book is dedicated to my mom.

Thank you for teaching me the real meaning of boundaries.

You can be amazing
You can turn a phrase into a weapon or a drug.
You can be the outcast
Or be the backlash of somebody's lack of love.

Or you can start speaking up.

From the song 'Brave' by Sara Bareilles (2013)

Acknowledgment

In bringing this book to life, I have been blessed with an abundance of love, support, and guidance from some truly incredible souls.

To my amazing husband, Brian: You were the first person in my life who encouraged me to share my voice, and your love and support over the years have given me the courage to reach farther than I ever could have imagined. Thank you for choosing to share this journey with me and for being the voice of reason when I need it.

To my incredible coach, Vanessa: Your wisdom, guidance, and unwavering belief in my abilities have been a guiding light over the years, and honestly, I owe so much of who I am to your thoughtful and wise guidance. Your steady hand and compassionate heart have helped me navigate the craziness in my life for well over a decade and always help to keep me focused on the journey ahead. Thank you for always holding a safe space and for calling me out on my bullshit.

To my wonderful friends and family: Your love, laughter, and unwavering support have meant the world to me. Thank you for lifting me up, cheering me on, and reminding me that I never walk this path alone. Special shout out to my amazing nieces, Jessica and Adyson, and my incredible nephews, Jordan and Matthew—I am so proud to be your 'Auntie Jen.'

Last, but certainly not least, to all my clients: Your trust, faith in me, and willingness to embark on this journey of growth and healing together have been nothing short of transformative. Each of you has taught me invaluable lessons, and I am deeply grateful for the privilege of walking alongside you on your path to healing and self-discovery.

Thank you to each and every one of you who has touched my life in ways big and small. Your love, support, and belief in me have made all the difference. We have created something exceptional together, and I am forever grateful for your part in this beautiful journey.

Finally, to you, the reader of this book: Thank you for trusting me with your time, energy, and attention. It's an honor to be part of your journey, and I hope that the words in these pages resonate with you and inspire meaningful change in your life. Your willingness to show up, dive deep, and explore new perspectives is a testament to your courage and commitment to growth. I am truly grateful for the opportunity to connect with you in this way, and I'm cheering you on every step of the way.

xo

Jen

Contents

Acknowledgment	vii
Preface	1
Welcome, Fellow Nice Person!	1
Chapter One	7
Moving Beyond Niceness	7
Chapter One Activity	15
Quiz: Just How Nice Are You	15
Chapter Two	19
Discovering and Rewriting Your Story	19
Chapter Two Activity	25
Telling Your Story	25
Chapter Three	27
Getting to Know Who You Are	27
Chapter Three Activity	35
Accessing Your Intuition	35
Chapter Four	37
Your Perception versus Experience	37
Chapter Four Activity	43
Hakalau—A Path To Inner Calm	43
Chapter Five	47
Boundaries and the Nature of Reality	47
Chapter Five Activity	55
Building Your Energetic Boundary	55
Chapter Six	59
Peeling Back the Layers to Find You	59
Chapter Six Activity	67
How Is That A Problem	67
Chapter Seven	71
The Problem Of Projection	71
Chapter Seven Activity	77
Neutralizing Your Triggers	77
Chapter Eight	85
The Art of Being Self-ish	85
Chapter Eight Activity	93

What Lights Up Your Soul	93
Chapter Nine	**103**
Where You End and Others Begin	103
Chapter Nine Activity	**119**
Where Do You End and Others Begin?	119
Chapter Ten	**123**
Conditions versus Boundaries	123
Chapter Ten Activity	**131**
Exploring Your Expectations	131
Chapter Eleven	**137**
Stop Telling People How You Feel	137
Chapter Eleven Activity	**147**
It's Time to R.A.G.E.	147
Release Anger Gain Empowerment	147
Chapter Twelve	**155**
Mastering the Art of Internal Boundaries	155
Chapter Twelve Activity	**167**
Creating Your Internal Boundaries Playbook	167
Chapter Thirteen	**171**
The Boundaries Blueprint	171
Chapter Thirteen Activity	**191**
Mapping Out Your Boundaries	191
Chapter Fourteen	**199**
The Art of Compassionate Negotiation	199
Chapter Fourteen Activity	**207**
Exploring Compassionate Negotiation	207
Chapter Fifteen	**211**
Offering Compassionate Feedback	211
Chapter Fifteen Activity	**223**
Becoming a Feedback Fan	223
Chapter Sixteen	**227**
The Flipside of Boundaries: Receptivity	227
Chapter Sixteen Activity	**237**
The "I Would Love" Exercise	237
Chapter Seventeen	**241**
When Sh*t Goes Sideways	241

Chapter Seventeen Activity 245
    Putting It All Together 245
Conclusion 249
    Healing The World 249
    About the Author 253
    References...255

PREFACE
Welcome, Fellow Nice Person!

"Setting boundaries is your responsibility. You get to decide what is and isn't allowed in your life."-Unknown

Welcome! And congratulations. If you are reading these words, you are (or at least think you might be) part of an elite and growing group of individuals considered '*Nice.*' You likely have a few close friends, possibly even a supporting circle of acquaintances, family members, and co-workers, who describe you as their "go-to" person. You may even have a reputation for being the kind of person who loves to help out.

Who can always be relied on to lend a helping hand.

Who is never more than a phone call away.

And who will Never. Ever. Say. No.

For so long, I was this person. I would do anything for anyone. And the truth is, I really do enjoy helping others. It gives me so much joy to watch someone's face light up, knowing that I was a part of it and that I made someone's day a little brighter and more manageable. I am a natural helper, and it honestly never occurred to me that I could say no!

But here's the problem: In all my eagerness to say 'Yes' to everyone else, I forgot about saying 'Yes' to me.

Oops.

And that's where it all went wrong.

In the beginning, it was subtle, you know? I was a little less interested in the things I used to love, a little less vibrant. A little quieter. But I was still doing what I needed to do, and I "put on a brave face" and soldiered on.

Because that's what we do, isn't it?

But over time, the changes became more profound. I found myself avoiding the activities I used to enjoy, and those once-beloved hobbies began to feel like burdens. It was as if I had become a stranger in my own life, performing a role that wasn't written for me.

Eventually, the physical problems started: chronic sinus infections and colds, minor aches and pains, and just a general feeling of blah.

And the fear. Oh, the fear.

It seemed overnight I became scared, anxious, and afraid of, well, everything! Things I had handled so easily in the past began to overwhelm me, and I just wanted to crawl into a warm, dark hole and hide.

Forever.

Being 'Nice' looks so wonderful from the outside, it's no wonder it's the thing we all strive for! But it turns out we were all sold a bill of goods because living like this—always "on," always smiling, never rocking the boat, being 'Nice'—is slowly killing us. The good news is change is possible and I am proof that healing your life from the inside-out can happen and is way easier than you may think.

So, who am I? I am someone who has walked the path of brokenness and lived to tell the story. I am someone who has experienced a dark night of the soul and lived there for over a decade. I am someone who has been told, over and over again, that I am broken.

And yet here I am. Stronger than before.

So, from one *'Nice'* person to another: Welcome, and thank you for being here.

Over the following chapters, I am going to introduce you back to *You* and to the parts of yourself that maybe haven't been acknowledged in a very long time. And by the time we are done, you will have the knowledge, skills, and tools you need to begin a more profound process of personal healing and transformation guided by the supportive and wise presence of boundaries.

Welcome to your journey.

How to use this book:

This book is designed to walk you step-by-step through the process of creating healthier boundaries in your life and is best read in order, as each chapter builds on the last. As you progress, you might be tempted to skip over some of the chapter exercises. Pay attention, because the ones that make you the most uncomfortable are the ones you likely need the most. To get the most out of this experience, I recommend fully participating and giving yourself the gift of diving in wholeheartedly.

Here's what we are going to cover:

How to access and use your emotions as powerful tools for feedback and growth.

How to master the art of setting clear, effective boundaries with yourself and others using the Boundaries Blueprint.

How to neutralize your triggers and turn the biggest jerks in your life into your best boundary-setting allies.

How to use compassionate negotiation to navigate tricky or difficult conversations with empathy and understanding.

How to offer effective feedback in a way that strengthens relationships using the Feedback Formula.

How to be more receptive and cultivate authentic gratitude in your life.

How to stop being '*Nice*' and start creating a life that inspires both you and those around you.

Signs You Need Better Boundaries

Still on the fence about whether or not you actually need better boundaries in your life? Here are some signs that the boundaries you have are no longer working for you:

You often say "Yes" to others, even when everything inside you is urging you to say "No."

You bend over backward to keep others happy, even at the expense of your own well-being.

When someone hurts or frustrates you, you keep quiet, bottling up your feelings and storing away unspoken thoughts.

You prioritize everyone else's needs over your own and often feel burned out, overwhelmed and exhausted.

You constantly agree to others' demands while your own energy and time are stretched thin.

You feel like you have to walk on eggshells and hold back your true thoughts and opinions to avoid conflict.

You often feel overlooked, unappreciated, or like you don't quite belong in social settings.

You hesitate to ask for help, fearing you might be a burden to others.

You struggle to say "No," even when you are feeling overwhelmed, because you don't want to disappoint anyone.

You feel guilty for taking time for yourself, as if you should always be available for others.

You believe you need to earn love and approval by constantly giving, doing, or being "perfect."

You often put your own dreams and desires on hold to support others in achieving theirs.

You find yourself constantly apologizing, even when it's not your fault, just to keep the peace.

You feel responsible for other people's happiness, often at the cost of your own.

You notice that you often end up doing more than your fair share, whether at work or in personal relationships, because it feels easier than saying "No."

Final Thoughts

Letting go of being 'Nice' is one of the best gifts you can give yourself, and learning to show up compassionately is the starting point of an incredible healing journey.

You in? Good!

Let's do this.

Bonus Stuff

As a thank-you for picking up *How To Set Boundaries (Without Feeling Like a D*ck)*, I have created two bonus tools to help support you on your boundary-setting journey:

01/ A Guided Meditation to help you stay grounded and centered as you work through the book. You can use this meditation anytime, and once you've explored Energetic Boundaries in Chapter Five, it will become an even more powerful tool for protecting your energy.

02/ A Workbook designed to supplement the exercises in the book, making it even easier to apply what you've learned.

To access your free gifts, visit www.btgwellness.com/book, click the link, and fill out the form to have your tools sent straight to your inbox!

MOVING BEYOND NICENESS

CHAPTER ONE
Moving Beyond Niceness

"Nice is a decision. Compassion is a lifestyle." -Covey

Let's start at the very beginning (a very good place to start!) and begin by asking a simple question: how '*Nice*' are you?

If your ultimate goal is to master the art of boundaries and become a true boundary-setting warrior, then the first step is to recognize how being overly '*Nice*' and habitually putting others' needs ahead of your own can quietly erase you from your life.

In this chapter, my goal is to show you why offering genuine compassion, rather than relying on relentless people-pleasing, is the key to a better and more balanced way of living.

The Problem with Being Nice

If you're anything like me, you are probably wondering, what's so wrong with being '*Nice*'? I mean, isn't that what we're supposed to be? From a very young age, we're told by parents, teachers, and everyone around us to *Be nice, Play nice, That's not nice,* and *Ask nicely.* We're taught that being 'Nice' is the key to being liked, accepted, and valued in society. So, isn't being 'Nice' the ultimate goal?

Well, not really.

You see, being 'Nice' requires you to put other people first—to always be available for their wants, needs, and desires. And that's great! For them. But when we spend so much of our time focusing on what other people want and need, it's really easy to completely forget about ourselves in the mix.

And that's a *problem*.

As someone who considers herself a highly sensitive and naturally empathetic person, I know how easy it is to get caught up in taking care of others. I have a deep capacity to sense the emotions and needs of those around me, and I genuinely love offering support wherever I can. It feels good to be there for others—to help, to listen, to comfort. It's a beautiful gift, and I'm grateful for it. But here's what I've learned: even the most empathetic heart needs boundaries, and if I'm going to use my empathy as a superpower, I need to make sure I'm just as attuned to my own needs as I am to everyone else's, don't you think?

And see, that's the rub. That's the problem with being 'Nice' and having no boundaries: it ultimately requires you to abandon your wants and needs in servitude to the wants and needs of other people. It makes you super cool and chill to be around, and it will slowly erode your sense of self until you have nothing left to give.

Ouch.

The alternative, and what I hope to show you throughout this book, is how to be compassionate instead. How to use your knowledge of *Who You Are* to show up more authentically, love more deeply, and share more vulnerably.

You see, being 'Nice' is, well, nice. But being compassionate leaves space for you to exist as well.

And that's always better.

So, why should you listen to me – what makes me an expert on boundaries? The truth is, I learned how to navigate my way through the choppy waters of healthy communication and boundaries by sheer necessity and desperation. Growing up, I was taught that emotions were silly. That talking about your feelings was just bullshit psychobabble and that the only good and acceptable emotions were happiness and laughter—which means I learned to laugh a lot and am pretty damned funny if I do say so myself.

Growing up, I was taught that love—LOVE—meant never being angry or upset, always giving the other person the benefit of the doubt, and being willing to give in to keep the peace no matter what the personal cost or sacrifice. And so, I learned to stuff my emotions down. To turn them off and rationalize them away. To hide them from myself and others.

In other words, I learned to be '*Nice.*' Which is kind of the default in society, isn't it?

Let's be honest, many of the significant dogmatic themes of this historical period revere the philosophy of martyrs—the idea of sacrificing yourself for some greater good, of suffering now for rewards later.

This is all well and good, but spoiler alert: the martyr dies in the end.

Yikes.

And I get it because this is what I was taught, too, and as a result, I never really learned to trust myself. I think I feared that if I allowed myself to open up, even just a crack, like Pandora's box, everything would come tumbling out, and I would be suffocated and consumed by a tsunami of emotions.

So, I learned to ignore my feelings; to push them down, and rely purely on my logic and rationale to get me through.

And it totally worked!

Until it didn't.

Because here's what I've learned about our emotions: the more we try to ignore them, the more stuck we get because they never really go away, do they? They just go into hiding.

They go underground.

Have you ever walked into a room after an argument or conflict and sensed that something was off? Like, a visceral or noticeable tension in the air? I call it *Pissed Mist*. There's a residue that strong emotions leave behind and, when they are not acknowledged, this energy begins to infect everything.

And it will eventually start to consume you.

That's what happened to me.

My Story: From Broken to Unbreakable

By the age of two, I was already learning how to be codependent and give up my own needs and opinions to please others. By the age of 5, I was starting to show symptoms of severe anxiety and self-injury. But it wasn't until I was 19 that things got really bad for me, and that's when I received my official diagnosis:

- Anorexia
- Bulimia
- Major Depressive Disorder
- Generalized Anxiety Disorder
- Obsessive Compulsive Disorder
- Suicidal Ideation
- Self-harm (which means, yes, there are scars on my body that I put there).

In other words, broken.

Every doctor I saw and every specialist I consulted all agreed: I was broken. And, in many ways, they were right. Because when a lot of very smart people, with a lot of impressive degrees on the wall and letters after their names, tell you you're broken, how long until you begin to believe them?

Growing up, I don't remember feeling broken. In fact, I had what I thought was a relatively normal childhood. From the outside, my family appeared affectionate and united—albeit with a touch of eccentricity. But as time passed, I began to notice inconsistencies that

HOW TO SET BOUNDARIES (WITHOUT FEELING LIKE A D*CK)

puzzled and confused me. Feelings that didn't make sense, fears that had no basis.

Or so I thought.

As a child, I could sense something was off about my family, but I could never quite put my finger on it. As an adult, I learned that my mother lived with a personality disorder, which made emotional resilience and genuine connection exceptionally difficult for her. Despite her struggles, she still longed for the closeness and family she didn't have growing up. While she did her best, much of the time her best was chaotic and sometimes downright scary. It could be fun and crazy, but it was also terribly confusing and lacked the kind of stability a young child needs to feel safe and loved.

And so, I began to break.

A lot of people think eating disorders are about weight or getting attention and, while this certainly plays a part, consider this: a person with anorexia uses their conscious willpower to override their body's own built-in self-preservation mechanism. It is a slow suicide, a death by a thousand paper cuts. It is about fear and control; it is about self-loathing and shame. Anorexia is born of a profound and persistent desire to destroy and obliterate the self. To disappear from existence—literally. Trust me when I tell you that the level of pain and shame required to starve yourself is not the result of not having a flat tummy or wanting to be a size 2. It comes from a much deeper, much darker place.

I know. I've been there.

With each passing day, the pressure continued to build until the pain became unbearable and the fear began to consume me. I finally broke down. And that's when we decided it was time for me to go to the hospital.

Those moments in the hospital come to me in spurts and flashes, movies of a lifetime that seem so foreign and long ago. But still, some memories remain. I remember sitting under one of those old TVs they used to have screwed into a corner on the wall (these were the days before flat screens and smartphones), and I remember wishing it would fall on me so the pain would stop. I remember meeting with the on-call psychologist, a scrawny little guy with wire-rimmed glasses and a bowtie. I remember the scratchy feel of the hospital gown against my skin and how I liked it and found it comforting. I remember my dad going to a local donut shop at 3 a.m. and bringing back a batch of fresh-from-the-oven cheddar biscuits.

And I remember Dwayne, an incredible soul who was part of the hospital's Crisis Team (a team I would meet many more times over the coming years). He was the first person to acknowledge me.

To notice <u>me</u>, not just my pain.

He was the first person who told me I was not broken, but it would take another decade of pain and darkness to fully understand his message.

It wasn't until I learned about a beautiful Japanese art form called *Kintsukuroi* that things began to click into place for me.

Unbroken: Stronger Than Before

Kintsukuroi (keen-tsoo-koo-roy), which translates to 'heal or repair with gold,' is the Japanese art of repairing broken pottery pieces with molten gold or silver, in essence highlighting the scars of the break. Rather than attempt to hide the injury or pretend it never happened, it was understood that the piece was more beautiful for having been broken and healed. These newly repaired pieces still held the essence of the original, but with something new added. While they weren't whole in the same way as before, they were no longer broken either.

They were, what I call *Unbroken*—stronger than before.

The ancient practice of Kintsukuroi taught me that our scars aren't something to hide, but rather something to embrace as they are proof of our resilience and ability to rebuild and grow stronger. Just as a broken bone cannot break in the same way again, these repaired pottery pieces become more valuable and stronger with their unique golden seams. Similarly, as we heal, we too become stronger and more capable through the challenges we've overcome.

HOW TO SET BOUNDARIES (WITHOUT FEELING LIKE A D*CK)

In 2010, I walked away from my eating disorder and began my journey back to health. And it all started when I stopped being *'Nice'* and embraced a new way of showing up.

It all started with boundaries.

MOVING BEYOND NICENESS

HOW TO SET BOUNDARIES (WITHOUT FEELING LIKE A D*CK)

CHAPTER ONE ACTIVITY

Quiz: Just How Nice Are You

It's time to find out just how 'Nice' you really are. Are you at a healthy level of 'Nice', or are you on the brink of a full-scale, nuclear 'Nice' meltdown of epic proportions?

Complete the quiz below to find out!

Step One: For each of the questions below, answer with either Yes or No:

1. Do you consider yourself 'Nice'?
2. Are you great at putting everyone else's needs first but forget about yourself in the mix?
3. Have you ever wondered, "If I'm taking care of everyone else—who is taking care of me?"
4. Are you always willing to lend a helping hand to others while your projects are left untouched?
5. Do people describe you as a "go-to" person or the one with all the answers?
6. Do you feel like you are being taken advantage of or are too understanding for your own good?
7. Do you like feeling needed?
8. Do you find yourself constantly apologizing and justifying yourself?
9. Do you find yourself agreeing with or saying yes when you don't want to and then feeling resentful afterward?
10. Are you great at avoiding confrontation—at all costs?
11. Do you consider yourself 'easygoing' and often think it's not worth speaking up and 'rocking the boat'?
12. Do you struggle with feelings of depression, anxiety, or overwhelm regularly?

MOVING BEYOND NICENESS

13. Do you often volunteer to help with tasks or responsibilities, even when overwhelmed?
14. Do you have difficulty saying 'no' to requests, even when you lack time or energy?
15. Do you prioritize others' happiness and comfort over your own?
16. Do you feel guilty when taking time for yourself or prioritizing your needs?
17. Do you frequently ignore or suppress your emotions to avoid conflict or discomfort?
18. Do you often feel drained or exhausted after social interactions or helping others?
19. Do you struggle to stand up for yourself and communicate your needs?
20. Do you feel responsible for solving other people's problems or fixing their issues?
21. Do you have difficulty asking for help or support when you need it?

Step Two: Add up the total number of Yeses.

0-5: You are definitely *Nice*, but it is probably still manageable. You likely feel a wide range of emotions and are decent at speaking up and getting your needs met. For you, this book will introduce you to tools to help prevent you from wandering down that dark road of severe *Niceness*. And you may just gain some new perspectives on yourself or someone else in your life.

6-10: You are teetering between being a healthy level of *Nice* and wandering into the world of *Too Nice*. This is a caution zone where you need to be alert to any indications of getting too comfortable putting yourself last. For you, this book will help keep you from falling over the edge and give you ways to identify if, and when, it is time to bring in extra reinforcements.

11-15: You are really *Nice* and likely pride yourself on being this way. You likely feel it is your duty to sacrifice for the people you love and possibly struggle with knowing where to begin when setting healthy boundaries without feeling overwhelming guilt. For you, this book will serve as an essential step on your journey to healing your relationship with YOU and will open up new perspectives on how to offer kindness without sacrificing your needs.

16-21: Warning! Warning! We have a toxically Nice person! Chances are you are either walking around secretly, seething mad all the time, or you have so skillfully removed anger from your world that you may barely feel anger at all. If you can't remember the last time you got good and pissed off—welcome. I am so glad you are here because this book is your wake-up call and your path back to a life filled with all the richness and joys of connection.

MOVING BEYOND NICENESS

CHAPTER TWO

Discovering and Rewriting Your Story

"Knowing yourself is the beginning of all wisdom." –Aristotle

Let's begin by jumping in and considering a very important question: Why are you here?

Often, in our effort to meet others' expectations, we can lose sight of who we really are and why we're here, which is why it's important to take a step back, clarify our intentions, and examine the story we tell ourselves.

In this chapter, I want to dive a little deeper and explore the importance of understanding your personal story and how it plays a pivotal role in shaping your identity and guiding your life.

So, why are you here?

No, really. Why. Are. You. Here.

I know your life is busy, and I know you could be doing anything right now, so why are you here? What brought our paths together? What made you decide to start reading this book right here, right now? What are you hoping to find?

Whether you've dabbled in mindfulness, set business goals at work, or are just beginning your journey with boundaries, you likely already know that having a clear intention is key to getting where you want to go. After all, you can't reach your destination if you're not sure where you're starting from or why you're headed there, right?

So, why are you here?

Maybe your life is unraveling at the seams, and you're just fed up and exhausted from the constant struggle. Or maybe everything seems to be going along quite fine, thank-you-very-much, but you sense there's something more and you are looking for some new perspectives. Maybe you're on a quest of self-expression and self-understanding, and this just sounded like the next logical step.

Or maybe you're not entirely sure why you're here. Maybe you were simply guided here by a series of seemingly random coincidences and just happened to find yourself here, in this moment, reading these words. Whatever the reason you are here, welcome. And thank you for being here. You have chosen to embark on a truly remarkable and profoundly healing journey that has the potential to elevate every aspect of your life.

And it all begins with this simple question: Why are you here?

When you ask yourself this question, you begin a profound voyage of self-discovery, and when it comes to establishing and respecting healthy boundaries, self-awareness is key.

So, why are you here?

When Fear Stopped Being Enough

When I first began my journey of self-discovery, I, too, was at a crossroads in my life. On the surface, everything seemed fine—I had a decent job, good friends, and a family that loved me. But deep down, I felt a persistent emptiness; a nagging sense that something was missing.

By this point, I had already spent years bouncing from therapist to therapist, each time eager and hopeful to find the secret to creating a life I wanted to live. And each time, feeling more and more hopeless when

HOW TO SET BOUNDARIES WITHOUT FEELING LIKE A D*CK

I was ultimately deemed too broken to ever feel good. It wasn't until I met my coach that things actually began to turn around for me. In our first session, she pinpointed something that 13 years of therapy and a four-year degree in Psychology had never addressed. And it all started with the simple question: "Why are you here?"

Honestly, at first, I didn't even know how to answer her, but the question stuck with me. With her support and guidance, I learned to take a long, hard look at my life and I began to question the stories I had been telling myself. I realized that much of my inner narrative had been shaped by the expectations of my family and a need to please others.

I had internalized so many external voices that I had lost touch with my own.

While it wasn't always a comfortable process, as I started to peel back the layers, I discovered that healing old wounds and confronting my triggers was much easier than I had been led to believe. For the first time, I started truly listening to my inner voice, and the more I did, the more positive effects began to ripple through other areas of my life in subtle but profound ways.

I remember one night, just a few months after I started working with my coach, I was sitting on the sofa watching TV with my husband, when a commercial for *Canada's Got Talent* came on—a spin-off of the hit American and British talent competitions. By then, I had been singing for years, but always in private where no one could hear me. Aside from the odd karaoke night fueled by 'liquid courage,' the only person who had ever actually heard me sing was my husband who accidentally walked in on me belting out a power ballad one day.

As we watched the commercial, my husband turned to me and said, "You know, Jen, you should totally audition for that." While his words were encouraging, my immediate response was, "No way—I'm way too chicken for that!" But as soon as the words left my mouth, something shifted inside me. It was like an epiphany and suddenly a new thought bubbled up: Is that really the only reason? And if fear is the only reason, is that enough anymore?

It was a profound turning point for me as it was the first time I ever thought to question the story I was telling myself.

In that moment I finally saw just how much I had let fear control my life and I decided that it would no longer be enough to keep me from going after what I wanted. That simple realization changed everything and it marked the beginning of a journey I honestly never thought I'd have the strength to take. Through the wonderful support of my coach, I began to rewrite my story. I learned to set healthier boundaries, not just with others, but with myself as well, and I learned how to listen to my emotions and learn from them. I finally stopped letting fear, guilt and obligation dictate my actions and, instead, I started honoring my true desires.

Oh, and I did end up auditioning for *Canada's Got Talent* after all! While I didn't make it past the first round (my knees were shaking so badly, it's a wonder I was able to make any sound at all!), the real victory was finding the courage to change the story I was telling myself. Despite the fear, taking that leap was a pivotal moment in my life and it opened the door for me to explore other avenues that brought more singing and music into my life.

While the transformation didn't happen overnight, the more I replaced the rigid conditions in my life with healthier, more flexible boundaries, the more aligned with my authentic self I felt. My relationships improved, my sense of purpose became more clear, and I began to feel a more profound sense of satisfaction and fulfillment.

Having walked this path I have learned that everyone has the power to rewrite their story and create a life that genuinely reflects *Who They Are* at their core. But first we need to acknowledge the story we are starting with.

So, what is your story?

The Stories We Tell Ourselves

We all have a story don't we? It's that thing we tell ourselves, about ourselves, to ourselves. It's that constant running narrative that plays in the background of our every waking moment; the *talky-talky*, chattering little voice in our head that can make us feel like we're going crazy. While it can be tempting to dismiss the stories in our head as meaningless noise or believe they have no significant impact on our lives—what if that's not true?

HOW TO SET BOUNDARIES WITHOUT FEELING LIKE A D*CK

What if your story runs deeper than you think?

In the 2004 book, *The Hidden Messages in Water*,[1] Dr. Masaru Emoto, a Japanese researcher and scientist, discusses his findings on the effects of various thoughts, intentions, and beliefs on the molecular structure of water. In his most famous work, he exposed samples of water from the Fujiwara Dam in Japan to various stimuli, including words, music, thoughts, intentions, and emotions. He then flash-froze the water using a unique process to observe the resulting ice crystals under a microscope.

The result? When the water was exposed to positive, loving words and intentions, it produced a beautiful and symmetrical ice crystal pattern, much like you would see if you looked at snowflakes under a microscope. But, when the water was exposed to harmful words and intentions, the symmetry suddenly disappeared and the water molecules appeared distorted and disorganized.

Although Dr. Emoto's work has faced skepticism from some in the scientific community, it does bring up an interesting question: How deep does your story go?

If the human body is made up of between 60% to 80% water[2] (depending on your age and hydration level), and if different thoughts, beliefs, and intentions impact the molecular structure of water—what would you look like if we put you under the microscope? Would the story you tell yourself weave a beautiful and intricate pattern of symmetry and balance? Or would it be disorganized, and chaotic, and a bit of a mess?

Whether you realize it or not, your story matters. The things you say to yourself in your head are not meaningless noise; they are woven into the very fabric of *Who You Are* and are a reflection of your experiences, beliefs, and unique perspectives. Your story shapes how you perceive the world and how you experience your sense of self. But—and here's the key—it doesn't define you permanently.

Which means you have the power to change it.

By intentionally understanding and sharing your story you can learn to create a more meaningful and authentic life that truly reflects *Who You Are*. And if your goal is to create healthy boundaries, starting with the words you use with yourself is a key step that is often skipped or ignored.

Too often, I hear people try to erase or deny their story, attempting to bury it under false platitudes or pleasantries. For example, someone might say, "My friend is being rude to me lately, which really hurts my feelings and, frankly, pisses me off, but I know they're probably just stressed out and I shouldn't let it bother me, so I've decided to just let it go."

Which is great—I'm all for letting things go—but the big question is: when you let something go, where does it go? Is it really gone, or have you just hidden it from yourself and buried it underground where even you can't find it?

We'll talk more about this later.

The bottom line is, you are not meant to deny your story, ignore it, or try to stuff it down and pretend it never happened. And you are not meant to stay silent in the name of people pleasing or being *'Nice.'* Instead, you are meant to learn from your story and use it as a stepping stone to something bigger and better.

A true boundary journey involves excavating the depths of *Who You Are* and reclaiming every part of yourself without fear or shame. It's about owning your truth and embracing a new perspective.

And that's why you are here, isn't it?

This book is about learning to use boundaries as the starting point for an exquisite journey of profound healing, and your story is where it all begins.

So, what's your story? What have you been telling yourself?

And what would happen if you could change it?

It's time to tell that old story once and for all.

CHAPTER TWO ACTIVITY
Telling Your Story

It's time to put pen to paper and get your story out—because this is the last time you'll ever need to tell it in its current form. By writing down where you're starting from on your boundary journey, you can acknowledge the past and set the stage for a brighter future.

In this activity, I want you to take a moment to write down your story one last time. By the time you have finished this book, you will have started the process of creating a brand new story for yourself—one that truly honors *Who You Are* and is protected with compassionate, healthy boundaries.

This activity is a three-part process and should take less than five minutes. All you need is a pen, your journal or a notebook, and a few minutes to yourself.

Step one: Write your story in a single paragraph

In this step, I want you to write your current life story in a single paragraph. This is not the story you want or wish you had. This is your current story, the one you want to change; the one that might be kind of crappy and noisy and chaotic and dark. Feel free to be as messy as you need to be as you honor where you are starting from.

Step two: Edit your story down to a single sentence

Once you have written out your story in paragraph form, the next step is to distill it into a single sentence. This one sentence should encapsulate your story's overarching theme or main struggle.

Step three: Summarize your story in a single word

In this final step, I want you to condense your story further by summarizing it in a single word. That's right—I want you to honor your story with just one word. This word should represent the essence of your story and capture its fundamental nature.

For example, my word would have been *Broken*.

DISCOVERING AND REWRITING YOUR STORY

Remember: This is the last time you will ever have to tell this old story. By completing these three steps, you not only validate your current story, you take an important first step towards rewriting a new one.

While it may seem simple, this exercise can serve as a powerful catalyst for transformation and self-reflection and can help pave the way for a deeper exploration of your identity, purpose, and potential—which are essential steps when creating and sharing healthy boundaries in your life.

In the next chapter, we will go a little deeper and explore *Who You Are,* how you fit into the world, and just how deep that old story went.

CHAPTER THREE

Getting to Know Who You Are

"The journey of discovery begins not with seeking new landscapes but with having new eyes." -Marcel Proust

Congratulations on acknowledging the story you have been telling yourself. How did it feel to finally confront the familiar words and themes that have shaped your life thus far? Did it feel freeing? Empowering? Or maybe even a bit uncomfortable?

If you haven't yet given yourself the gift of completing the activity from the last chapter, I highly encourage you to take a moment and go back and do it now. By courageously sharing your old story, you take an important step towards moving beyond the need to be *'Nice'* and into a space where healthy boundaries can begin to take root.

Which brings us to the next step on our boundary-setting adventure: discovering what makes you tick.

It's time to ask yourself, *"Who Am I?"*

In this chapter, I want to talk about the intricate workings of your brain and explore how your consciousness shapes your perception of reality. By understanding the interplay between the different aspects of your mind, you can gain a clearer picture of *Who You Are*. And while it might seem strange to ask such a philosophical question in a book about boundaries, this understanding is key and forms the foundation for everything else.

So, who are you?

What makes you—you know—*You*?

Take me, for example. My name is Jennifer, but most people call me Jen. I am a Master Hypnotherapist, Emotional Resiliency Coach, Mentor, and Instructor and I specialize in helping people, from all walks of life, both individually and in groups, overcome feelings of overwhelm, anxiety, and past trauma by helping them bridge the gap between their head and their heart.

Of course, I wear many other hats in my life as well, like being a wife, an aunt, and a fur-mom to my fabulous fur family. In my spare time, I love golfing, curling (yep, I'm Canadian through and through) and I love to sing. Fun fact: I'm also a hula hoop dancer (or 'Hooper' as we call ourselves), and I always have at least two hula hoops in my car at all times—yes, seriously! But surely, *Who I Am* is goes beyond these labels, right? I mean, even if you were to strip away all these titles, the core "*Me*" would still be there, wouldn't it?

Finding Out Who You Are

Years ago, I attended a networking event where we were challenged to introduce ourselves without mentioning our name, job, title, or family relationships, so we couldn't say things like "I'm a mom" or "I'm a nurse." While I initially dismissed this as a silly icebreaker game, I was surprised at how profound it ended up being for me.

The first person who stood up introduced themselves as a quiet poet and a kind-hearted soul who loved animals and rock music. The next person described themselves as a talented painter who also loved to play the accordion and bake cupcakes. As each person shared their unique identity, I felt my nerves building—I still had no idea what I was going to say. But, surprisingly, when my turn came around and I stood up, the words just popped out of my mouth:

HOW TO SET BOUNDARIES WITHOUT FEELING LIKE A D*CK

"I am a Star Trek loving, hula hoop dancing, a cappella singing, hippy-nerd."

It felt like a personal revelation! Sharing who I was in this way was so much more meaningful than just saying my name or my family role or my job title and, to this day, this is still my favorite description of *Who I Am*.

Often, we become so attached to the labels and roles we play in life that we forget to connect with the deeper part of ourselves that is always present. Through all the bumps, bruises, and changes—beneath all the roles and titles you wear—there exists a Core Essence; a stable anchor that endures. This *You* is not defined by your job, name, or title; it's your true self and it persists even when all else is stripped away. Nurturing and understanding this part of yourself is critical as it is this inner core that your healthy boundaries aim to protect.

By safeguarding the Core Essence of *Who You Are*, you ensure that your true self remains safe, respected, and intact amidst the various roles and labels you take on in life.

From a psychological perspective, it can be very helpful to understand that *Who You Are* is the result of an intricate interaction between two distinct parts of your mind: your conscious mind and your unconscious mind. This concept of self has origins in Freudian theory, introduced in the late 19th and early 20th centuries by Sigmund Freud, the pioneer of psychoanalysis.

Freud's groundbreaking theories, particularly his exploration of the unconscious mind, played a profound part in shaping our understanding of the intricate inner workings of the human psyche.[3]

Think of your brain as a theater production. On the stage, in the spotlight, is your conscious mind, which represents the part of your mind that you're aware of; the part that directs your thoughts and actions. Meanwhile, backstage is your unconscious mind, quietly managing all the intricate processes behind the scenes to keep everything running smoothly, even though you're not aware of it. Just like a play depends on both the actors in the spotlight and the crew backstage, our identity is shaped by both our conscious and unconscious minds.

Your Rational Mind

When I talk about your conscious mind, I am referring to anything that you are aware of at any given moment. For example, right now, you are likely aware of the words you're reading on the page and the feel of this book or device in your hands. But what about the sensation of your clothes on your body? Or the rhythm of your breathing? Or the hair on your head?

Only now that I've mentioned these things, I bet you're noticing them, right?

So, where was all that information a moment ago? Your body has been processing it the whole time, yet only a small fraction of it made it into your conscious awareness while the rest stayed in the background, processed unconsciously. But by simply shifting your focus, you were able to bring new sensations and information into the spotlight of your conscious mind.

Neat, right?

Your conscious mind is linked to the newer, more evolved parts of your brain, specifically the cerebral cortex, or what I like to call the "*thinky-thinky*" brain. This part is essential for your thoughts, with different areas handling various aspects of thought processing. For instance, the prefrontal cortex, located right behind your forehead, is heavily involved in planning, decision-making, and problem-solving, while the temporal lobes help with memory formation and retrieval, allowing you to recall past experiences and information.

Within the cerebral cortex is the frontal lobe, where the magic of your conscious awareness happens. In fact, it's likely your frontal lobe that's engaged right now, helping you understand these new concepts and focus on the words on this page. This part of your mind excels at managing the details and minutiae of life and is designed to constantly scan your environment, compare it to past experiences, and use that information to try and predict possible future scenarios. Its goal is to identify and anticipate problems, believing that by understanding why something is happening, it can ensure our survival.

Unfortunately, your conscious mind can get stuck in problem-finding mode, becoming so focused on identifying issues that it can struggle to recognize solutions. It's kind of like having a passenger who points out every flaw in your driving but never quite helps to navigate. This is why we can spend so much time trying to figure out the "*Why*" behind our problems, only to see them getting bigger.

Your Emotional Mind

Your unconscious mind, on the other hand, is a very different place. Where your conscious mind is logical, linear, and uses language to communicate, your unconscious mind is more instinctual, primitive and symbolic. It's associated with much older structures of the brain, like the limbic system, and operates on associations and feelings.

Your unconscious mind is like a little hoarder, obsessively collecting memories, emotions, and desires while also stashing away anything you don't want to face or don't know how to deal with. In fact, whenever you "push something out of your mind," this is where it goes. Every time you rationalize your emotions or try to talk yourself out of them, they don't actually go away; they just move from your conscious awareness into your unconscious mind, effectively making them harder for you to find and address.

Have you ever put something away for safekeeping only to never find it again? That's sort of what happens when we bury our emotions—we hide them so well in our unconscious mind that even we can forget they exist. These unresolved emotions linger just beneath the surface of our awareness, and turn into the triggers that keep us feeling stuck and frustrated.

In other words, when we ignore our emotions, we're only setting ourselves up for them to come back later, often even stronger.

Oops.

Your Intuitive Self

If you ever needed proof that the universe has a sense of humor, here it is: the same unconscious mind where you hide things you don't want to deal with is also home to your intuition and gut instinct.

GETTING TO KNOW WHO YOU ARE

Your unconscious mind functions like your own personal *'spidey-sense,'* constantly analyzing your environment and picking up on subtle changes long before your conscious mind catches on. This part of your mind is what allows you to make sense of your world and give it meaning. It detects subtle nuances and patterns that your conscious mind might overlook and guides you with intuitive instincts and gut feelings.

This continuous background analysis not only helps you navigate complex situations but also enriches your overall experience of life by providing a deeper connection with your surroundings. While your logical mind helps you navigate daily life, your instinctive mind helps give your experiences depth and meaning.

In her compelling TED Talk, *My Stroke Of Insight: A Brain Scientist's Personal Journey*,[4] neuroanatomist Jill Bolte Taylor shares the remarkable story of her stroke, which offers a unique window into the workings of the different aspects of the human brain. On the morning of December 10, 1996, Taylor describes experiencing a severe hemorrhage in the left hemisphere of her brain. As a brain scientist, she talks about how she was able to observe, in real-time, as her brain functions, including motion, speech, memory, self-awareness and the ability to perceive reality, completely deteriorated, one by one.

Taylor describes an incredible shift in her consciousness between two distinct realities: the logical, analytical, detail-oriented world of the left-brain, and the intuitive, expansive, kinesthetic world of the right-brain. As her left hemisphere shut down, she describes how her ability to engage in structured, conscious activities like walking, talking, reading, and recalling memories also disappeared. Meanwhile, her right hemisphere brought feelings of euphoria, peace, and interconnectedness. A state of pure nirvana.

Taylor's story beautifully illustrates how the different aspects of our minds work together to shape our perception of reality and our greater sense of self. Her journey highlights the importance of embracing both aspects of our mind to fully understand and appreciate *Who We Are*.

So, who are you?

HOW TO SET BOUNDARIES WITHOUT FEELING LIKE A D*CK

You are a complex and sometimes messy interplay between different parts of your mind: your conscious mind, which focuses on what you think, and your unconscious mind, which encompasses what you feel and believe. This dynamic interaction between your thoughts and feelings—your head and your heart—creates the wholeness of *Who You Are* and shapes how you perceive the world around you.

Understanding this complexity is the first step toward achieving deeper self-awareness. And since your boundaries are meant to protect your true self, the better you understand *Who You Are*, the more effective your boundaries can be.

GETTING TO KNOW WHO YOU ARE

CHAPTER THREE ACTIVITY
Accessing Your Intuition

Before we go any further, I want to take a moment to help you connect more deeply with your intuition and unconscious mind by teaching you how to tap into the power of your imagination. Believe it or not, your imagination is a powerful tool that can bring hidden sensations and emotions into your awareness and allow you to tap into insights and truths that are often just beneath the surface. This practice will help you better understand and trust the signals your mind and body are sending, setting the stage for the work we'll do together.

For this exercise, find a comfortable, quiet place where you can sit or lie down without distractions. Make sure you're in a safe environment where you can close your eyes and relax for a few minutes.

Step One: Extend either your left or right hand in front of you, palm facing up. Take a few deep breaths, inhaling deeply through your nose and exhaling slowly through your mouth.

Step Two: Close your eyes and imagine a small, 1-inch round pink glowing sphere of light resting gently in your outstretched hand. Imagine its warmth and the gentle weight it exerts on your palm. Imagine its vibrant pink glow, softly pulsing with light, and imagine any sounds it might make, like a gentle hum or a faint chime.

Once you have clearly imagined the sphere in your hand, raise your other hand in acknowledgment of this connection with your intuition.

When you are ready, relax your hands and open your eyes. Now, take a moment to reflect on this experience.

To deepen your reflection, ask yourself:

- How did you know when the sphere was there?
- What was the difference between the moments of "no sphere" and "yes, there's a sphere now"?

- Did you experience any physical sensations or emotional responses when you imagined the sphere?

When you did this exercise, you likely noticed a subtle shift, a quiet knowing that the sphere existed in your hand. This tiny shift, so faint it's like a whisper, is the sensation of your intuition. It's the feeling that isn't a feeling; the knowing that defies all logic. Although, intellectually, you knew there was nothing in your hand, engaging your imagination activated your unconscious mind, allowing you to sense the sphere.

What's interesting is that MRI studies show our brains can't distinguish between real and imagined experiences so when you imagine a sphere in your hand, your brain responds as if it were real, causing subtle but noticeable shifts. This process activates the part of our mind that deals with abstract concepts and non-tangible realities and can help you learn to tap into your unconscious mind.

The more you practice using your imagination, the better you can get at picking up on the subtle hints of your intuition.

CHAPTER FOUR

Your Perception versus Experience

"We do not see things as they are, we see them as we are." - Unknown

In the last chapter, we explored *Who You Are* through the lens of psychology, but your identity isn't solely shaped by your psychological experiences. It's also profoundly influenced by your external perceptions and by what your neurology prioritizes from the massive stream of data constantly being collected by your unconscious mind.

In this chapter, we'll dive deeper into the world of perception and how it shapes your experience of reality.

This goes beyond just what your eyes see or your ears hear; it's about how your mind processes these sensory inputs to construct your own unique version of reality. By understanding how your brain filters sensory information, you can begin to shift your perspective and create boundaries that actually feel good to share.

The World Beyond Your Senses

Whether you are aware of it or not, in every moment, you are being bombarded with a massive amount of information. In fact, according

YOUR PERCEPTION VERSUS EXPERIENCE

to the Encyclopedia Britannica, the human body is exposed to somewhere in the range of 11 million bits of information every single second.[5] This information comes to you through each of your five senses and is made up everything you see, smell, taste, touch and hear.

From the moment your neurology first came online, you have been exposed to this infinite stream of sensory data. Information in the form of energy—such as sound waves, electromagnetic radiation, and tactile vibrations—streams in to all five of your senses simultaneously where it is first processed by your unconscious mind before moving into your conscious awareness. These sensory impressions are your only way of interacting with and knowing the world around you. Without them, you would be cut off from experiencing the world in any meaningful way.

Imagine you're walking down a busy city street. Your eyes take in the vibrant colors of storefronts, the movement of people, and the changing traffic lights. Your ears pick up the honking of cars, the chatter of pedestrians, and the distant sound of a siren. Your nose catches the aroma of freshly baked bread from a nearby bakery mixed with the faint scent of car exhaust. Your skin feels the cool breeze and the firmness of the pavement under your feet.

All this sensory data floods your neurology, creating a rich tapestry of impressions that shape your experience of each moment. The problem is, the human brain is only capable of consciously processing a tiny fraction of this incoming information at a time, with estimates putting it at around 50 bits per second. This means most of the sensory input we receive from our environment—whether visual, auditory, tactile, or otherwise—goes completely unnoticed by our conscious mind. In fact, the vast majority of those 11 million bits of information are filtered out and hidden in the background of your consciousness.

Even though your unconscious mind is still recording and processing this data, it remains out of reach of your conscious awareness. While this filtering process is helpful in allowing us to focus on what's most important in the moment, it also means that a lot of information goes unnoticed.

Hidden in Plain Sight

A few years ago, I found myself at the local drug store, searching for a very specific brand of eye drops that had been recommended to me. Armed with the product name and a picture of the package, I confidently approached the aisle where all the eye drops were displayed. I scanned the top shelf, then the middle, and finally the bottom shelves. There were all sorts of eye drops, but not the one I was looking for.

After a few minutes of fruitless searching, I decided to seek help and found one of the store associates to ask if they had the brand I was searching for. Without missing a beat, he walked me right back to the shelf I had just been staring at, pointed directly to the shelf at eye-level, and said, "There you go." And there they were—the exact eye drops I had been searching for, right in front of my face the whole time.

Sometimes, something can be right in front of us but still be completely out of our awareness.

Our environment is filled with an overwhelming amount of sensory information, and our conscious mind has to quickly filter through it all, deciding what to pay attention to and what to ignore. Your brain relies heavily on your unconscious mind to process, filter, and sort this incoming data using mental shortcuts, patterns and rapid associations. Since our brain can't pay attention to everything at once, it has evolved to play favorites through a process called selective attention. This allows your brain to sort through all the sensory chaos around you and zero in on what it thinks you need to know at any given moment.

Think about the last time you were at a noisy party. You could likely hear your friend talking despite the loud music and chatter around you, right? This ability to selectively pay attention to the environment is what allows you to focus on the conversation you care about while filtering out the background noise. While it's an efficient system for data processing, sometimes this filtering process messes up, and we miss what's right in plain sight.

YOUR PERCEPTION VERSUS EXPERIENCE

Years ago, I remember being in one of my psychology classes. There were about 50 students in this class, so it was fairly small compared to some of my other lectures. We were all paying close attention to what the professor was discussing, engrossed in the topic of the day. About 20 minutes into the class, a woman walked in wearing a bright blue business suit and carrying a briefcase—quite strange for a first-year psych class where the rest of us were decked out in sweatpants and carrying backpacks overloaded with textbooks. The woman came in, apologized profusely for being late, found a seat, and tried to get settled. However, as she was sitting down, her bag slipped and the coffee she was holding spilled all over her. She jumped back out of the chair, apologized again profusely, and left, presumably to clean herself up and die of embarrassment.

About 10 minutes after she left, our professor calmly handed out a pop quiz: "Tell me about the person who came into the classroom ten minutes ago. Was it a man or a woman? What color hair did they have? What color suit were they wearing? What type of items were they carrying? What type of drink did they spill?" Do you know that not one person in that room got every detail correct! Sure, some of us remembered a woman wearing a suit but couldn't recall the color or what she was carrying. Some remembered she had a Starbucks coffee, while others thought it was a man, not a woman. After the quiz, the woman came back into the room and introduced herself, and we all got to see just how much information we had missed. It was a startling revelation.

We humans think we are very aware, but the reality is most of what is going on around us never makes it through into our conscious awareness. While selective attention can help us pay attention to a conversation in a noisy party, it can sometimes cause us to miss obvious details. Luckily, we can train our brain to pay better attention to the things we want to experience in the world and take more control over what information makes it through our unconscious filters.

Your Inner Bouncer

Imagine your unconscious mind as the bouncer for an exclusive club. This bouncer is responsible for making sure only the right guests get in, keeping the atmosphere inside the club positive and enjoyable. Most of the time, your unconscious mind does a great job, but sometimes it gets confused and lets in the wrong crowd. When that happens, the club begins to fill up with unwelcome guests like other people's opinions, judgements or fears making it hard to enjoy yourself and find peace. To keep your club's atmosphere just right, you need to help your bouncer recognize who truly belongs and who to keep out.

How can you do this? The answer, of course, is boundaries.

Think of your boundaries as a VIP guest list for your brain. Just like a bouncer uses a list to decide who to let in and who to keep out, your unconscious mind uses your boundaries to determine which thoughts, opinions, and emotions are allowed to take up space in your life and what makes it past your brain's filters. By clearly defining what is and isn't acceptable in your life, you can shape your inner world and drastically shift your reality.

So, if you thought boundaries was just about saying 'No' without feeling guilty—think again.

YOUR PERCEPTION VERSUS EXPERIENCE

CHAPTER FOUR ACTIVITY

Hakalau—A Path To Inner Calm

As we dive deeper into understanding *Who You Are* and building solid boundaries, it's natural to feel a little overwhelmed. That's why I want to share with you a fantastic technique you can use anytime you are feeling anxious, upset, or mentally drained.

This exercise is adapted from Hakalau, a traditional Hawaiian meditation practice.[6] Hakalau means "*eyes wide open*," and it is an ancient technique that helps you focus and achieve a meditative state by tapping into your peripheral vision. Using this technique has been shown to induce alpha brain waves, which are associated with relaxed focus, learning and memory.

If you've ever been "*in the zone*" while doing something, this technique allows you to induce that feeling whenever and wherever you want it.

What I love most about this technique is that it can take you from feeling completely overwhelmed to feeling totally Zen in less than 2 minutes—no yoga mat required. It's also great for people who are new to meditation and need a quick way to feel more calm.

Feel free to use this technique whenever you're doubting yourself, overthinking, or having trouble relaxing due to an overactive mind. It's also highly effective for calming down during a full-blown panic attack and is an excellent resource for students who struggle with learning differences, attention challenges, and test anxiety, as it can help improve focus and reduce stress.

Here's how to use this technique:

Step One: Turn Your Eyes Up

Keeping your chin parallel to the floor, turn your eyes up and find a comfortable spot on the ceiling or wall to look at.

The key word is *comfortable*—there is no need to try to look at the back of your own brain. If anything hurts or feels uncomfortable, just

YOUR PERCEPTION VERSUS EXPERIENCE

lower your gaze a bit. Remember to keep your chin level and only move your eyes up, fixing them on your spot to anchor your focus. Feel free to blink as this is not a staring contest.

Step Two: Breathe and Go Deeper

Take a deep breath, and as you exhale, imagine focusing on the very center of your chosen spot, concentrating all of your attention on that point, to the best of your ability.

Take another 1 – 2 breaths here.

Step Three: Shift Your Awareness

As you continue to focus on your spot, notice that your awareness will naturally begin to shift and spread out. Without doing anything at all, notice that you can now become aware of your peripheral vision. Gradually allow your awareness to spread out around you while keeping your gaze anchored on your spot.

Step Four: Wrap the Awareness Around You

Continue expanding your awareness until you reach the edges of your peripheral vision, usually around where your ears are. Once you've reached this point, use your imagination to extend your awareness even further, wrapping it all the way around and behind you.

Imagine you can see everything behind you, hear all the sounds, and feel the space surrounding you—as if your awareness is enveloping you 360 degrees.

Step Five: Breathe and expand

Take a few more breaths here, staying in this state for as long as you want. As your awareness broadens, notice how your thoughts can begin to fade into the background and your breath can begin to regulate.

When you're ready, take one more deep breath in and, as you exhale, bring your eyes back down.

Now, take a moment to notice what's different. What feels, sounds, or looks different to you? What can you observe in this state of gentle focus and awareness? Many people report experiencing very visceral sensations using this technique. Some feel calmer and more centered, while others notice the room somehow appears bigger or brighter or that sounds are more pronounced or muffled.

Know that whatever you experience is perfect.

Tip: If you use this technique during a full-blown panic attack, be aware that your body will fight you and resist keeping your eyes up. That's okay! Do whatever you can to keep your eyes open and looking up at your spot until you can catch your breath, and then continue with the rest of the technique.

Free Resource:

If you would like to hear an audio recording of me walking you through this process, you can find a free download in the Free Resources section of my coaching website: www.livelifeunbroken.com

YOUR PERCEPTION VERSUS EXPERIENCE

CHAPTER FIVE

Boundaries and the Nature of Reality

"Reality is merely an illusion, albeit a very persistent one."
- Albert Einstein

Before we dive deeper into the nuts and bolts of boundaries, I want to give you another perspective to help you answer the question, "*Who am I?*"—because it really is that important.

In this chapter, we're going to break down your experience into four distinct layers of reality and explore how your physical senses, thoughts, emotions, and energy all interact to form your unique experience of the world. Learning to recognize and respect the differences between each of these layers can help you develop a more holistic approach to boundary-setting that doesn't require you to avoid people or shut down to keep the peace.

The Four Layers of Reality

Imagine being able to paint a broad picture of yourself, organizing all aspects of *Who You Are* into four distinct layers of reality: physical, mental, emotional and energetic. Each of these layers represents a unique dimension of your existence and, therefore, requires its own specific type of boundaries.

Let's go through these one at a time.

The Physical Layer of Reality: This layer of reality includes everything you can perceive with your five senses and is made up of all the things you can see, smell, taste, touch and hear. In your body, the physical layer of reality includes things like your bones, skin, organs, tissues, and all the physical '*stuff*' that makes you, You.

Boundaries on the physical layer of reality are relatively straightforward, thanks to the clear definition provided by your trusty body. I mean, you wouldn't look at someone else's elbow and wonder, "Hmmm... is that mine?" On the physical layer of reality, it's pretty obvious where you end and someone else begins.

The Mental Layer of Reality: This layer of reality is made up of your thoughts, logical reasoning, and conscious awareness. It includes the internal dialogue you use to make sense of all the information you encounter in the physical world.

This is where your story lives, which we explored in earlier chapters. The mental layer of reality serves as the observer of your experiences but is not the experience itself. Experiences happen in your body, within the physical layer of reality, when your senses detect stimuli, such as the warmth of the sun, the sound of laughter, or the taste of a ripe strawberry. This sensory information is neutral and has no inherent meaning; it is just data.

Since we can only be consciously aware of a small fraction of this information at a time, your conscious mind acts like a diligent analyst, observing, interpreting, and evaluating this filtered and fragmented data and then weaving into a coherent story to help you understand and navigate your world. It is this mental layer of reality that comes up with stories like, "The sun feels warm on my skin because it's a beautiful summer day," or "The laughter sounds joyful because my friends are happy."

By creating these inner dialogues, your conscious mind helps you understand your experiences and weave them into your broader life story.

HOW TO SET BOUNDARIES (WITHOUT FEELING LIKE A D*CK)

Boundaries on the mental layer of reality involve recognizing that your thoughts are uniquely yours; they are about having standards around how and when you share your unique thoughts, feelings and opinions. These boundaries are primarily designed for ourselves, and we will explore them more in later chapters.

The Emotional Layer of Reality: This layer of reality encompasses your feelings, memories, values, and beliefs. It retains a record of all the experiences you've ever had and is closely associated with your unconscious mind, which manages these experiences behind the scenes. This layer is where we infuse the stories created by our conscious mind with a rich and vibrant tapestry of emotions, giving each experience its own unique shade and depth.

Think about the last time you had to make a tough decision. While your head likely weighed all the pros and cons, your heart probably guided you with feelings and intuition. For instance, when deciding whether to take a new job, you might use logic to make sense of all the details, but your emotions—how you feel about the people, the place, and the work—also play a significant role in your decision.

In addition to connecting us with the deeper, more emotional aspects of *Who We Are*, the emotional layer of reality is also linked to our most instinctive, ancient selves and holds the imprint of what is known as the collective unconscious. This concept, first introduced by Swiss psychiatrist Carl Jung, refers to the part of the unconscious mind that is shared amongst beings of the same species.[7]

Jung believed the collective unconscious to be a reservoir of shared experiences, containing archetypal patterns and universal symbols. He proposed that it holds knowledge passed down through generations, and that these deeply ancestral patterns influence our behavior and emotional responses, even if we are not consciously aware of them. The emotional layer of reality, therefore, is not only a personal reservoir of our own life's experiences but also a gateway to this deeper, shared heritage.

Boundaries within this layer of reality are extremely important because they help you navigate both your individual emotions and the collective imprints you carry. By understanding and respecting these boundaries, you can better handle your emotional responses and distinguish your feelings from those of others, as well as from emotions inherited through generational trauma. When people talk about setting healthy boundaries, this is the layer of reality they are usually talking about. But boundaries here are not just about sharing your feelings or saying 'No' to others. Healthy boundaries on the emotional layer of reality are meant to help you identify what you truly need to feel safe, respected, and fulfilled. Once you have this clarity, your job is to then communicate these desires effectively to create relationships that are both meaningful and balanced.

These are the types of boundaries we will thoroughly explore throughout this book.

The Spiritual/Energetic Layer of Reality: Finally, we have the spiritual or energetic layer of reality. Now, when most people hear terms like "energetic" or "spiritual," they tend to think of things like angels, spirit guides, ghosts, or other mystical concepts. While those elements can certainly be part of it, this layer is also where your inspiration and highest aspirations reside.

Think about the last time you had a sudden spark of clarity—an "Aha!" moment or a breakthrough that shifted your entire perspective. Where do you suppose these flashes of insight come from? Some of humanity's most profound insights and breakthroughs have come from beyond our immediate physical, mental and emotional reality. They tap into something bigger—the energetic layer—where they lie in wait for the right moment to emerge into our consciousness. It is this layer that connects you to a broader universe of possibilities and helps you tap into deeper levels of creativity, intuition, and knowing. While this layer might include the mystical and the mysterious, it's also a very real part of your everyday life and offers moments of inspiration and insight that can profoundly impact your life's journey.

Recently, I watched a documentary about Stephen Hawking, the renowned theoretical physicist, and his groundbreaking theories on the nature of the universe. Hawking was describing a time when he was stuck on a complex equation, and despite his relentless thinking, he couldn't figure it out. Just when he was about to give up, he describes experiencing a sudden spark of insight, like a lightning bolt; a moment when everything suddenly just clicked into place. This epiphany led to his groundbreaking theories on the nature of black holes and their role in the creation of our known universe.

Hawking's ideas were groundbreaking; completely revolutionary and far outside the box of accepted thought at the time. These new concepts didn't yet exist in physical reality as published papers or studied topics. They didn't emerge from the mental layer of reality as pre-existing thoughts, nor were they part of the collective unconscious or emotional realm. Instead, these flashes of insight came from the realm of inspiration and higher thought—the energetic layer of reality.

The Quantum Field of Potential

In quantum physics—the branch of physics that deals with particles smaller than an atom—there's a fascinating theory that suggests that all possibilities, outcomes, and phenomena coexist simultaneously in a vast, infinite field of potential.[8] According to this theory, everything that has ever happened, will ever happen, or could ever happen is already present in this limitless field. To better understand this concept, let's explore one of the most famous experiments in quantum physics: the double-slit experiment.[9]

(Warning: I'm about to get a little nerdy here but I promise, if you stay with me, it will all make sense!)

First performed by Thomas Young in the early 19th century, the double-slit experiment is a ground-breaking experiment that shows how subatomic particles like electrons or photons can exist in multiple states at once—a phenomenon known as *superposition*.

In the double-slit experiment, subatomic particles are fired, one at a time, towards a barrier with two narrow slits in it while, behind the barrier, a screen detects where each particle lands. When only one of the slits is kept open, the particles pass through and create a single band impression on the screen behind, as expected. However, when both slits are open, something surprising happens. Instead of creating two bands, the particles, instead, form an interference pattern, acting more like waves that overlap and interfere with each other. These results were baffling to scientists. How can particles switch from behaving like individual particles to acting like waves?

In an even more surprising plot-twist, when detectors are placed at the slits to observe which slit each particle passes through, they revert back to behaving like individual particles. It's as if the particles know they are being watched! This phenomenon, known as *The Observer Effect*, suggests that the mere act of measuring or observing subatomic particles can collapse the quantum wave function causing the particles to choose a definite path and position.

Think of it like this: Imagine the quantum field like a huge library filled with countless books, each one representing a different possible story of your life. All of these stories exist simultaneously, but you can only read and experience the one you pick up.

The double-slit experiment suggests that reality is fluid and is shaped by our perceptions and conscious interactions. While this might seem like an unusual topic for a book about boundaries, it's actually highly relevant. Your boundaries, it turns out, are like a lens through which you view and interact with the world; they determine what you let into your life and what you keep out, effectively shaping your personal reality.

By establishing healthier boundaries, you not only make it easier to get your needs met, you also become a deliberate creator of your life.

Your Energetic Boundaries

Have you ever found yourself thinking, "I can just feel that person is judging me," or "I can sense that my boss is really upset with me"? In those moments, when you're attempting to understand or anticipate what someone else is thinking and feeling, whose energetic space do you suppose you are in? Are you in your own, or have you drifted into theirs?

It turns out, every time you prioritize someone else's emotions or thoughts over your own, you temporarily leave your own energetic space and step into theirs. While this is a natural part of human interaction, doing it too often can mean you're spending more time

HOW TO SET BOUNDARIES (WITHOUT FEELING LIKE A D*CK)

immersed in other people's energetic space than in your own. And that's a problem.

What exactly do I mean by *'energetic space'*?

Imagine your energetic space as an invisible force field that completely surrounds you in a large, protective bubble. This bubble is big enough that if you were to stretch your arms out to the side, your fingertips would just brush the inside of the bubble, still safely within its protection. Imagine that this bubble extends above your head and beneath your feet, enveloping you completely. This force field, or energetic boundary, represents your *sphere of influence*. Within this space, you have some measure of control over your environment, while what lies outside your bubble is generally beyond your influence and, therefore, beyond your realm of control.

Do this: reach your arms out as far as they can go and try to grab something on the other side of the room. No matter how much you may want that thing, notice that because it is beyond your immediate grasp it is beyond your ability to influence and control without bringing in outside help (like asking someone to hand it to you).

The same principle applies to your personal boundaries; anything outside your immediate space is more likely to be beyond your control. Your energetic space, therefore, represents your sphere of influence in the world.

Your energetic boundary is designed to protect you from being drained by annoying coworkers, rude strangers, or what I like to call other peoples' *oogedy-boogedy bad vibes*. They allow you to interact with the world without feeling overwhelmed or drained and they help you maintain your inner peace, even when you're surrounded by chaos. As a matter of fact, if being around negative people leaves you feeling burned out and exhausted, it might be because you haven't focused enough on maintaining your energetic boundaries.

In addition to keeping other people's *ick* vibes out of your space, your energetic boundaries are also designed to contain all aspects of *Who You Are*, across all the other layers of reality. This includes your physical body, thoughts, feelings, desires, beliefs, opinions, emotions, dreams, aspirations, and everything else that contributes to the entirety of *Who You Are*. Which makes your energetic boundaries pretty darn important, don't you think?

Often, in our efforts to be accommodating, considerate, or simply '*Nice*,' we can unintentionally let other people's thoughts, opinions, judgments, criticisms, moods, and emotions seep into our personal space. But here's the thing: if your energetic space is filled with other people's emotions and opinions, is it really still your own space?

Hmmmm...

Imagine you share a house with a roommate, and every day they leave something small in your room: a few coins, a pair of socks, or their forgotten keys. Over time, your room will start to feel less like your own space and more like a chaotic mix of your stuff and theirs. This is basically what happens when we let other people's judgments, opinions, and emotions into our energetic space—it stops feeling like our own.

When we are constantly tuning into other people's emotions and trying to read their thoughts it's like being a radio that is picking up every station at once. Sure, you're hearing it all, but you're not able to really understand anything. Worse, the noise can make it hard to hear your own signal.

The good news is that creating energetic boundaries is extremely easy, and you don't need to have any awkward conversations to do it.

This means you can start right away.

HOW TO SET BOUNDARIES (WITHOUT FEELING LIKE A D*CK)

CHAPTER FIVE ACTIVITY
Building Your Energetic Boundary

Learning to tune into your energetic space is really easy—but it does require more than just a cognitive awareness. Luckily, your body's neurology comes with its own built-in mechanism to allow you to explore the world beyond the range of your physical, mental, and emotional realities.

That's right—it's your imagination.

In this activity, you'll use your imagination to create a vivid, three-dimensional impression of your personal space, making it easier to recognize and maintain your energetic boundaries.

A quick note about your imagination: when people first learn this technique, they often worry if they can't "see" or "feel" anything, so I want to assure you that connecting with your energetic boundary isn't about visualization or intuition—it's about engaging your neurology through a process of *active imagination*.

For example, if I asked you to imagine a rose, it might involve picturing the flower in your mind's eye or imagining the smell of its beautiful fragrance or the softness of the petals. It might even involve hearing the song *The Rose* by Bette Midler or *Bed of Roses* by Bon Jovi playing in your head. Or, you might simply think to yourself, "Yup, I'm imagining a rose."

All of these would be perfectly fine ways to imagine a rose.

Similarly, imagining your energetic space doesn't have to be visual. In fact, you can start by simply telling yourself that you're surrounded by a protective bubble that blocks out other people's thoughts and *ick* vibes. That's enough.

Over time, you can practice engaging your other senses if you want but, at the end of the day, this is your space and your imagination so however you imagine your energetic boundary is absolutely perfect.

Step One: Grounding

To begin, close your eyes and take a deep breath in and then exhale slowly, doing your best to release as much tension as you can. Do this a few more times, allowing yourself to begin to relax.

As you continue to breathe consciously, imagine tiny roots beginning to grow out from the bottoms of your feet. With each exhale, imagine these roots extending deeper and deeper into the earth, weaving through layers of soil and rock, growing stronger and more resilient with every breath. Keep doing this until your roots reach the large, dense crystal at the very center of the earth's molten core.

(Fun fact: Research suggests that the earth's core likely contains a very dense, iron-based crystal. Feel free to look it up if you're curious!)

Once your roots reach the crystal at the Earth's center, imagine wrapping them around it to connect with the powerful Earth energy.

This process is called *Grounding*.

Why is grounding important? Humans are naturally fragile, squishy creatures and, for us, the safest place tends to be close to the ground. Let's face it, even a fall from a very low height can cause significant injury and damage to our tissues. As a result, our neurology tends to feel safest when we are as close to the ground as possible. Lucky for us, our brains cannot distinguish between real and imagined scenarios, so simply imagining yourself connected to the Earth is enough to activate your parasympathetic nervous system—the part responsible for rest, relaxation, and digestion—and send your brain the message, 'I am safe.'

Step Two: Drawing Up Energy

Once you have used your imagination to connect to the Earth's energy, imagine you can now draw that vibrant energy up through your roots—as if you're pulling it through a straw—and into the soles of your feet. With each inhale, imagine you can pull this energy higher and higher, allowing it to fill your legs, belly, and chest, flowing into your shoulders, down your arms, up your neck, and finally reaching the very top of your head.

HOW TO SET BOUNDARIES (WITHOUT FEELING LIKE A D*CK)

Take as much time as you want with this step.

Step Three: Creating Your Bubble

When the energy reaches the top of your head, take a deep breath in and, as you exhale, imagine the energy bursting out through the crown of your head, cascading around you like a beautiful fountain of light. Continue to breathe in and out, using your imagination to draw the Earth's energy up through your roots and letting it flow out the top of your head until the fountain of light begins to form a protective, shimmering bubble that completely surrounds you.

Allow yourself to become aware of your bubble extending to your left and right, in front of you, behind you, above your head, and beneath your feet. Notice that you can stretch your arms out to the sides and your fingertips just gently brush the inside of the bubble, keeping you safely protected within.

Step Four: Adjusting The Energy

Once you have established your energetic boundary, it's important to make sure only what you want remains inside. Remember—this is your space, and you get to decide what stays and what goes.

Take a moment to notice if there's anything in your space that doesn't belong, like someone else's judgments or criticisms. Gently ask these to leave your bubble, using your imagination to clear your space of anything that isn't yours.

Finally, invite anything that belongs to you to return to your bubble and welcome it back into your space. This could include things like your courage, strength, patience, or even your sense of joy and creativity. By doing this, you reclaim your personal power and ensure your energy is fully aligned with *Who You Are*.

Feel free to complete this process as quickly or as slowly as makes sense for you. Sometimes, I have completed this process in under a minute, and other times, it has taken me nearly twenty. The amount of time you spend is entirely up to you, as long as you follow all the steps.

To end this practice, take a final deep breath in and out, and when you're ready, gently open your eyes.

Once you have defined your energetic space, this impression stays active in your neurology for around 24 hours, so be sure to repeat this practice daily for maximum benefits and effect.

NOTE: While this process might seem like a meditation practice for when you're alone, it's actually designed to help you tune into your energetic boundaries.

Once you get the hang of it, you can use it anytime, anywhere—even in emotionally or energetically tough situations. So, the next time you find yourself in an awkward or toxic environment, before doing anything else, imagine your roots grounding you and your bubble surrounding you. You can even do this while talking to someone else—in fact, I recommend it! This way, you can stay protected, even when dealing with other people's *oogedy-boogedy* ick energy.

Free Resource:

If you would like to hear this process as a guided meditation, you can find a free audio download in the Free Resources section of my coaching website: www.livelifeunbroken.com

CHAPTER SIX

Peeling Back the Layers to Find You

"Who looks outside, dreams; who looks inside, awakes." - Carl Jung

Now that you're familiar with the different layers of reality, I want to introduce you to one more approach to help you better understand *Who You Are*.

In this chapter, we will explore your Core Essence—the true You we are aiming to protect with better boundaries. This is the part of you that exists beneath all the childhood programming, all the baggage, and all the dramas and traumas. By connecting with this essential part of *Who You Are*, you can better identify the places in your life where you need healthier boundaries.

The Onion Model of Healing

When people talk about personal growth, they often compare it to peeling back the layers of an onion. While it might sound a bit cliché, this metaphor is actually a helpful way to understand the importance of healthy boundaries. Just as peeling an onion reveals new layers, setting better boundaries can help you uncover your true self, one layer at a time.

Imagine, for a moment, that you are an onion. At the very center of this onion is your Core Essence— your most aligned self, the perfection that defines *Who You Are*. When we are born, this Core Essence is all that exists and we come into the world perfect, whole, worthy, lovable, and enough.

I mean, have you ever looked at a newborn baby and thought, "Wow, what a worthless piece of crap"? No—of course not!

From the very beginning, we are beautiful and imperfect, carrying an inherent sense of worthiness and wholeness within us. But then, somewhere along the way, usually when we are very young, we begin to receive the message that *Who We Are* isn't okay. We might be told, in subtle and even not-so-subtle ways, that *Who We Are* is not enough, not worthy, not lovable, not wanted. We learn that our very existence makes other people feel uncomfortable—likely because it requires them to change, adapt, and grow their own boundaries to accommodate our existence.

In the process of them trying to adjust, we can accidentally internalize the belief that somehow we are to blame for their discomfort; that *Who We Are* is fundamentally flawed.

The First Layer: Shame and Self-Doubt

When we come to believe that there's something inherently wrong with us, it creates a deep wound that envelops our Core Essence in a layer of shame, self-doubt, and feelings of inadequacy. This protective layer shields us from further hurt, but also keeps us from truly knowing or expressing our authentic selves.

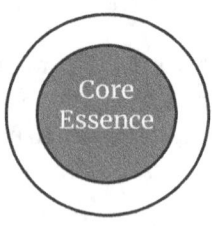

This shame and inadequacy come to the surface any time we are dismissed, ignored, or have our needs go unmet, and we will go to great lengths to keep it hidden from anyone or anything that might get too close to it—including ourselves. Deep down, we're terrified that our worst fears and deepest shames will be exposed.

These are the struggles we keep hidden; the parts of ourselves we don't want anyone to see. Our darkest secrets.

Back in high school, I remember taking an advanced physics class filled with incredibly smart, gifted students. Even though I was a straight-A student, I always felt like I didn't quite fit in. Afterall, I was smart, but these kids were gifted; exceptional and brilliant in ways I was not. I remember one group study session we were tackling a particularly challenging concept and everyone else seemed to catch on pretty quickly. I, however, struggled to keep up. While everyone was engaged in active discussions, I stayed quiet, nodding along and pretending to understand—but deep down, I was terrified that they would figure out that I wasn't as smart as them. That I didn't belong.

This shame that we experience can feel so real and so overwhelming that, eventually, we come to believe it is just an inherent part of us—that we are simply broken and damaged beyond repair. As this layer of shame grows, it distances us from our Core Essence and entangles us in the expectations and judgments of others, making it harder for us to recognize our own worth.

Over time, we can begin to lose sight of *Who We Are* and what we genuinely want. When that happens, the shame gets mixed up with our identity and we begin to think *Who We Are* is not okay.

The Second Layer: Fear and Anger

Since we mistakenly believe that the core of *Who We Are* is fundamentally flawed, living with this painful idea would be unbearable. To cope, we need to hide this layer of shame from ourselves so we can continue to live and function in society and the world at large.

And so, we create a new layer made up of Fear and Anger.

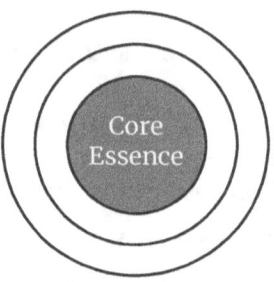

With this new layer, whenever someone gets too close or triggers our deepest wounds, we instinctively react. Anger becomes our shield, pushing others away, while fear becomes our escape route, causing us to shut down, run or hide. These emotions act as barriers, keeping the world at a safe distance and protecting us from feeling vulnerable.

But what happens when we want to build friendships, form intimate relationships, or just let someone get to know us? The vulnerability required for genuine connection will always risk exposing our deepest wounds, and without healthy boundaries, anger and fear will become our default defenses. While this might keep us feeling safe, it also makes our relationships messier than they need to be.

The Third Layer: Masks and Defense Mechanisms

When the anger and fear fail to keep our inner demons at bay, and we grow tired of feeling isolated from constantly fighting or running away, this is when we can begin to develop unhealthy coping mechanisms, social masks and even toxic behaviors designed to give the illusion of authenticity while keeping our true selves hidden.

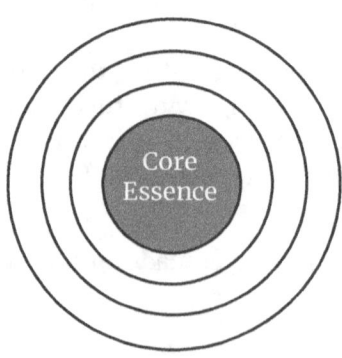

For example, we might become perfectionists and overachievers, constantly striving for recognition to gain approval. Or we might become the so-called '*class clown*,' using humor to deflect from our vulnerabilities. We might become codependent people pleasers, always fawning over others to feel loved. Or, we may turn into covert martyrs, trying to prove our worth by rescuing others. While these adaptive behaviors help us cope with confusing or painful emotions, they ultimately prevent genuine connection and keep us from forming truly authentic relationships.

When I first started my coaching practice, I worked with a client who had been diagnosed by her doctor with Borderline Personality Disorder (BPD). In addition to working with her therapist, she reached out to me to learn more about building emotional resilience. During our first session, my client shared with me that she felt trapped in an endless cycle of emotional outbursts and volatile relationships and she was convinced she was just fundamentally flawed.

Throughout our time together, we explored the onion model of healing and discussed how the BPD behaviors, though disruptive, actually served a protective purpose by keeping intense emotions, like shame, at bay. This new perspective made a huge difference and helped my client shift from feeling like a victim of her condition to feeling more in control of her life.

Through a combination of mind-body techniques, self-reflection, and coaching practices, my client learned how to reconnect with her Core Essence and, over time, began to realize she no longer needed those maladaptive behaviors in the same way—that *Who She Is* was enough. As my client practiced healthier communication techniques, she formed stronger and healthier relationships with just about everyone in her life.

While I'm not saying that boundaries can cure BPD—or any other diagnosis, for that matter—I do believe that developing a healthy sense of self and learning to protect it with healthy boundaries can significantly reduce emotional distress. Plus, it can make navigating the complexities of being human a whole lot less dramatic.

The Role of Addictions

What happens when our social masks and defense mechanisms still fail to keep us safe, and our inner shame continues to surface? What if, despite all the anger, fear, and coping strategies, our inner demons are still too much? This is when addictions can come into play, adding yet another layer to our onion.

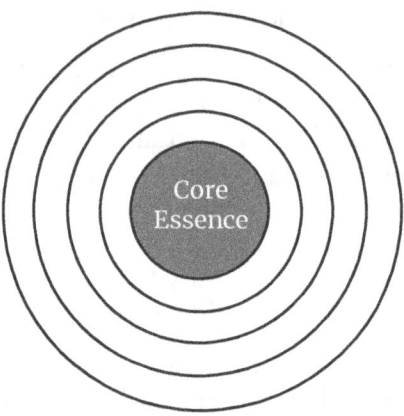

Addictions—whether to food, love, attention, social media, shopping, alcohol, or something more serious—are ways to numb the pain and distract ourselves from the shame we mistakenly think defines us. While addictions offer temporary relief, they prevent us from facing the real cause of our distress and trap us in a cycle of avoidance and pain. Worse, they delay the healing we need to truly reclaim *Who We Are*.

When viewed through the lens of the onion model, however, addictions can be understood as effective, albeit harmful, ways to cope with unresolved painful feelings. This perspective challenges the damaging notion that someone with an addiction is just inherently flawed or defective, which can perpetuate a victim mentality. Instead, it suggests that these adaptations—addictions, defense mechanisms, anger, fear, and shame—are simply protective layers built up over time.

HOW TO SET BOUNDARIES WITHOUT FEELING LIKE A D*CK

While these layers effectively keep our shame and deepest wounds hidden, they also distance us from our true, authentic selves. But, when you begin to set healthier boundaries, you can start to let go of your defenses, drop your social masks, and release the fear and anger that have been holding you back. In doing so, you can begin to reconnect with the Core Essence of *Who You Are*.

That's the magic of boundaries.

PEELING BACK THE LAYERS TO FIND YOU

CHAPTER SIX ACTIVITY
How Is That A Problem

Now that you're beginning to see how your problems can get buried under layers of unresolved issues, it's time to learn how to gently unearth these stuck emotions so you can move forward without the weight of the emotional baggage. Each time you try to outrun your emotions, push them away, or deny their validity, you add another layer to your onion, distancing yourself further from the truth of *Who You Are*.

This activity is designed to help you peel back those layers and uncover the beliefs that might be blocking your connection to your Core Essence. By simply asking and answering the questions in this exercise, you can gain valuable clarity on your most pressing challenges. To begin, grab your journal and find a space where you won't be disturbed for a few minutes.

Hint: This activity is designed to be straight-forward so avoid over-thinking! Simply write down the first thing that comes to mind when you ask yourself the questions.

Step One: Write down a problem. This could be a big problem or a small one—the choice is yours.

Next, rate the problem on a scale from 0 to 10, with 10 being "This is a big problem" and 0 being "This is not problem at all."

Step Two: Reflect on the problem and ask yourself, *"How is this a problem?"*

Write down your answer in your journal.

Repeat this three more times, each time reflecting on and asking the question about your most recent answer, not the original problem.

For example: Let's say the problem I want clarity on is, I can't seem to speak up in the moment. This is what I might write in my journal:

PEELING BACK THE LAYERS TO FIND YOU

Problem: I can't speak up in the moment.

How is that a problem? It's a problem because it means I look like an idiot and just stand there.

How is that a problem? If I just stand there, it's a problem because I'll look stupid.

How is that a problem? If I look stupid, it's a problem because then no one will want to hang out with me and I'll be alone.

How is that a problem? If no one wants to hang out with me and I'm alone that's a problem because it means no one likes me.

Notice how each time I'm asking the question based on the previous response, not the original problem.

Step Three: Using the last answer from Step Two, ask yourself, *"Where else in my life is this a problem?"*

Write down your answer in your journal.

For example: *Where else in my life do I believe no one likes me?* Everywhere.

Step Four: Now ask yourself, *"What has to happen for this problem to disappear?"*

Write down your answer.

For example: *What has to happen for me to know that people do like me?* They will invite me to lunch and ask me about my life.

Step Five: Finally, write down one thing you can do, starting immediately, to help make this happen.

For example: I can ask to join everyone for lunch.

Take a moment to reflect on your original problem and notice any changes. Rate the problem again using the same scale from 0 to 10, and make note of any shifts.

This activity may seem simple, but it is designed to help you gently peel back some layers and uncover hidden issues that have been concealing your authentic self. By following this process, you can begin to shift your mindset from focusing on problems to noticing solutions, allowing you to reconnect with more of *Who You Are*—which is the entire purpose of setting boundaries in the first place.

Feel free to use this technique whenever you're feeling stuck or need more clarity on a problem. You can also make it a part of your daily journaling practice if that works for you—the choice is yours.

PEELING BACK THE LAYERS TO FIND YOU

CHAPTER SEVEN

The Problem Of Projection

"Unless you learn to face your own shadows, you will continue to see them in others, because the world outside you is only a reflection of the world inside you." – Carl Jung

If you're still on the fence about the importance of creating healthier boundaries in your life, here's something to consider: When our boundaries are unclear, and we're busy being '*Nice*,' we unintentionally blur the line between *Who We Are* and the world around us. This results in layers of emotional baggage that not only obscure our Core Essence but also make it more likely for us to feel triggered by the people and situations we encounter.

In this chapter, I want to explore why other people can provoke such strong reactions in us and show you how to use their triggering behavior as a valuable mirror for your own personal growth and healing. By doing this, you can begin to transform the biggest jerks in your life into powerful catalysts for your own boundary journey.

THE PROBLEM OF PROJECTION

Everywhere You Go, There You Are

Think of your emotions like items you stuff into a closet. When life gets busy, you toss your feelings in there, promising yourself you'll deal with them later—but later never seems to come, does it? Over time, that closet begins to fill up, crammed full with all the stuff you've rationalized away, pushed aside or ignored, until it's so packed the doors won't even close. Eventually, just like an overstuffed closet spills its contents into the room, those unresolved emotions start creeping into your daily life. Suddenly, you're feeling overwhelmed, burned out, and anxious without even really knowing why.

To help manage this overflow, our unconscious mind has developed a way to reflect our unresolved issues onto other people, effectively forcing us to deal with them whether we like it or not. This adaptive mechanism ensures we can't run from our emotions forever. Unfortunately, it also means we sometimes react to other people based not on their actions but on our own unresolved feelings.

This happens through a process known as projection.

Projection is a concept that was first introduced by psychoanalyst Sigmund Freud and is based on the idea that what we don't address within ourselves will be reflected back to us by others.[10] Because we are so good at ignoring our feelings, either by rationalizing them or pushing them out of our minds, the only way for us to become aware of our unresolved issues is to see them reflected in someone else.

For example, let's say you're feeling jealous of a friend's promotion, but instead of acknowledging and processing your jealousy and finding healthy ways to channel this emotion, you instead dismiss your feelings by telling yourself you're being silly, illogical, or overly sensitive. This rejection of your own emotional experience is deeply damaging because it denies an important aspect of *Who You Are* on the emotional layer of reality. When you do this repeatedly, your mind has no choice but to unconsciously project those rejected feelings onto other people.

You might find yourself thinking your friend is actually jealous of you and may even accuse them of it. In this way, you don't have to face up to your own jealousy—instead, you see it as the other person's problem. This mechanism is helpful in allowing us to avoid dealing with our own difficult emotions but, as you can imagine, it can lead to a lot of misunderstandings and conflicts in our relationships.

The Role of Triggers

Any time we push down or rationalize emotions we don't want to deal with, those feelings don't just vanish into thin air. Instead, they linger in the recesses of our unconscious mind, waiting for something in our environment to trigger them back into our conscious awareness. These unresolved emotions then get projected onto the people around us, which, in turn, triggers us to face what we've been avoiding. Unfortunately, when this happens, we usually think our job is to suppress these feelings even more, or try to become less affected by them. What we don't realize is that these triggers are actually signals, guiding us to explore and heal what's been buried.

A few years back, we had some town workers come by our property to bury new lines for an internet provider. Before any digging started, the utilities and gas companies first came around and placed little flags throughout the yard to alert the workers to buried wires or other things underground that needed care or attention. Much like those little flags, your triggers are your unconscious mind's way of alerting you to where your unresolved issues are buried so you can find and heal them, instead of having to project them onto other people. While they may feel uncomfortable, your triggers are actually your greatest guides towards emotional resilience.

This means the commonly held belief that being triggered indicates something is wrong with us is completely false. In fact, your triggers are a sign that your unconscious mind is doing its job perfectly! It is simply bringing unresolved issues to the surface to be dealt with—which is exactly what it is designed to do.

The reality is, you were never meant to just "get over it" or push down your emotions indefinitely. Your emotional experiences are a vital part of *Who You Are*, and denying them isn't an option.

Since repressing emotions forever isn't safe or sustainable, our triggers serve as repeated opportunities to confront and heal what's been buried. And because they stem from our own unresolved issues or projected insecurities, it means everyone you meet essentially acts as a mirror, reflecting back to you all the parts of yourself you accept—as well as the parts you still struggle with. It is through these interactions with the people around you that hidden aspects of yourself are brought to light, offering you the chance to heal and grow.

So, that coworker who triggers you because they're always rude? It might actually be your projection because you're afraid of being perceived as rude by others. Or that neighbor who is always being so loud and judgmental? You might be projecting because you worry that others see you the same way.

Freud and Jung believed that projection happens because our conscious ego, which maintains our self-image, can't handle "unacceptable" feelings. To manage this, it buries these feelings under emotional layers and disguises them as traits in others. This mechanism helps us avoid the discomfort of self-recognition by seeing our issues reflected externally and allows us to keep functioning while avoiding the immediate pain of confronting our own inner demons.

The problem is, when we don't realize this is happening, our triggers and projections can cause misunderstandings as well as unnecessary conflict and drama in our relationships. We might find ourselves triggered and arguing with someone over their behavior, not realizing it's our own hidden feelings that we are projecting onto them. By recognizing projection for what it is, we can take responsibility for our own triggers and reclaim our projections, ensuring we create boundaries that are not driven by our past pain or traumas.

Projection in Action

Since we are so good at burying our pain and projecting it onto the people around us, it can be really hard to spot it happening in our own life. To help you more easily recognize where this might be showing up for you, let's explore some real-life examples inspired by some of my clients over the years. (Note: all names have been changed to protect privacy.)

HOW TO SET BOUNDARIES WITHOUT FEELING LIKE A D*CK

Sarah's Story:

Sarah, a project manager, often felt that her team didn't respect her. She was convinced that no one valued her contributions and she was on the verge of quitting her job. In our sessions, Sarah became more aware of the ways she was accidentally projecting her insecurities onto her team. Together, we focused on strengthening Sarah's own boundaries by learning to clearly communicate her needs without imposing conditions.

Over time, Sarah noticed a significant improvement in her work relationships and was pleasantly surprised by her team's positive response to her new approach. This transformation also boosted her overall confidence as the respect she sought from her team began to mirror the newfound respect she had for herself.

Maria's Journey:

Maria described herself as a caring and dependable person, but often felt let down by her friends. This constant disappointment left her feeling lonely and frustrated. As we worked together, Maria realized that her fear of being unreliable, rooted in a childhood of unmet parental expectations, was causing her to project these feelings onto her friends.

In addressing this, Maria started focusing on being dependable to herself first. She learned to set healthier boundaries around her time, became more punctual, and starting followed through on her commitments. To her surprise, she began to see her friends differently. It turns out they had been supportive all along, but her fears and insecurities had clouded her ability to notice it.

Jake's Revelation:

Jake, a devoted dad, often accused his partner of being unfaithful, even though he had no evidence to prove it. As you can imagine, this constant suspicion was creating a major rift in his relationship and his marriage was on the brink of a breakdown. Through our work together, Jake began to realize his accusations were actually stemming from his own guilt over a past relationship where he had been unfaithful.

Understanding this projection helped Jake take responsibility for his own insecurities and shame. He learned how to build trust and open communication with his partner and his relationship began to flourish. The baseless accusations disappeared and were replaced by a healthier, more trusting connection.

Quinn's Breakthrough:

Quinn, a dedicated palliative care nurse, often felt her coworkers thought she was incompetent. This feeling plagued her, making her angry, defensive and unmotivated to go to work. With support, Quinn began to understand that her feelings stemmed from her own self-doubt and imposter syndrome. Together we addressed her self-esteem challenges, and she started to recognize her skills and the positive impact they had on her patients.

By tackling her self-doubt head-on, Quinn stopped projecting her insecurities onto her coworkers and began to see her interactions in a more positive light. She came to understand that she was respected and valued just as she was.

Final Thoughts

As you can see, projection can really mess up our lives if we're not careful, and it can lead to unintentional misunderstandings and unnecessary drama.

Luckily, neutralizing your triggers and owning your projections is easier than you might think.

CHAPTER SEVEN ACTIVITY
Neutralizing Your Triggers

Now that you're beginning to understand the importance of recognizing when you're projecting, it's time to take the next step and learn how to turn the most triggering and challenging people in your life into powerful allies for setting healthy boundaries.

For this activity, grab a piece of paper and create a chart with four columns, like the one below. Then, think about the person in your life who triggers you the most and use them as the focus for this exercise.

Behavior	What It Gets Them	More or Less	Take Action

Column 1: Identifying Their Obnoxious Behavior

In this first column, jot down what it is about this person's behavior that really triggers you and ticks you off. Be brutally honest here; no sugarcoating allowed. You have my permission to use your most colorful language.

For example, let's say you're dealing with someone who's a pain-in-the-ass, know-it-all who has a short fuse and is a massive control freak, you would write down "Know-it-all," "Short fuse," and "Control freak" under the first column.

THE PROBLEM OF PROJECTION

Behavior	What It Gets Them	More or Less	Take Action
Know-It-All			
Short fuse			
Control freak			

Column 2: Figuring Out What It Gets Them

Next, consider what positive outcomes this behavior might be bringing the other person. People don't do things unless it serves them in some way, right? Which means even the most toxic behavior is motivated by a positive intention.

For example, a person who constantly seeks attention by throwing tantrums might be craving the validation they never received as a child. A coworker who dominates conversations and shuts everyone down might be trying to prove their worth and get noticed in a competitive environment.

Even if it's not immediately obvious, every behavior—no matter how toxic or annoying—serves a bigger purpose and has a positive intent behind it.

This doesn't mean these behaviors are okay or healthy, but it's important to recognize that how another person behaves is beyond your control. However, while we can't change what someone else is doing, we can use their behavior as a springboard for our own inner work and healing.

In this column, you get a chance to put on your thinking cap and consider why this person might be acting the way they are and what positive outcome they might be seeking through this behavior.

For the purpose of this example, let's use the following behaviors and their outcomes:

Validation and Being Right: A know-it-all always gets to feel superior and validated; they get to be right—even if it's only in their own mind. This behavior can stem from a need for self-assurance and respect.

Control and Getting Their Way: Someone with a short fuse might use their temper to quickly establish dominance and ensure they get their way. This could be a way to feel powerful and in control.

Being Heard: A control freak never has to worry about feeling left out or dismissed—they take charge to ensure their opinions are heard. This behavior often comes from a need for security and predictability.

Behavior	What It Gets Them	More or Less	Take Action
Know-It-All	Validation and be 'right'		
Short fuse	Control/Getting their way		
Control freak	Being heard		

Other positive underlying needs you might encounter include:

Self-Esteem: A person who frequently criticizes others may be trying to gain a sense of control or superiority in situations where

THE PROBLEM OF PROJECTION

they feel insecure. This behavior could be a way to bolster their self-esteem and help them feel respected.

Validation: Someone who is constantly interrupting during conversations might be seeking validation and acknowledgment. They could be trying to assert their presence and ensure their ideas and thoughts are heard and valued.

Acceptance: An individual who avoids conflict and always agrees with others may be striving to maintain peace and harmony. Their behavior might be driven by a need to avoid rejection or a desire to be liked and accepted by everyone around them.

Harmony: A person who lies frequently might be trying to avoid conflict or protect someone's feelings. This behavior could stem from a desire to keep the peace and avoid rocking the boat.

Power: Someone who procrastinates may be trying to manage their anxiety or fear of failure. By delaying tasks, they might be attempting to feel like they have more power to cope with overwhelming expectations and reduce their stress in the short term.

Again, no one is saying any of these behaviors are okay or desirable, but since we can't change other people, we might as well use them to better ourselves.

Let's move onto the next column.

Column 3: Do You Need More or Less

Once you have identified the possible positive intentions behind someone else's troublesome behaviors, it's time to apply that insight to your own healing journey. This is your moment for self-reflection. In the third column, revisit the positive intentions you noted in Column 2 and ask yourself if these are things you personally need more or less of in your own life. At this point, we are shifting the focus away from the other person, so be sure to reflect on this question solely in relation to your own personal growth.

Let's go back to our example from earlier:

If you were to decide that you need more "Validation and being right" in your life, you would go ahead and put a plus sign (+) in this column, indicating your need for more. If you decide that, in your life, you need less "Control and getting your own way," you could put a minus sign (-) in this column to symbolize that you need less. Similarly, if you were to decide you need more "Being heard," in your life, you would put another plus sign (+).

For each positive intention you identified in Column 2, reflect on whether you need more or less of that in your own life, and then mark it accordingly. By doing this, you are turning someone else's unpleasant behavior into a tool for your own self-discovery by identifying the traits you need to either embrace more or let go of.

Remember, you are evaluating each of these as they relate to your own personal journey, completely separate from the other person. The other person was just mirroring something back to you, highlighting it for your healing. Once you understand what this is, you can stop focusing on the other person and make this all about you.

Now, onto the final column.

Behavior	What It Gets Them	More or Less	Take Action
Know-It-All	Validation and be 'right'	+	
Short fuse	Control/Getting their way	-	
Control freak	Being heard	+	

Column 4: Do Something About It and Take Action

Identifying someone else's obnoxious behavior and recognizing how it is helpful is just the start. The real magic happens when you use this awareness to make tangible changes in your own life.

THE PROBLEM OF PROJECTION

In this final column, you get to explore the practical steps you can take to improve your personal development based on what you discovered in Column 3. Let's go back to our example again.

Let's say you recognized that you need:

- More (+) Validation and being right
- Less (-) Control and getting your way
- More (+) Being heard

Here's how you could achieve these goals:

More (+) Being right: One way to feel more 'Right' is to actually speak up and share what we want more often. By clearly expressing our needs, we can feel more validated and understood.

Less (-) Getting your way: One way to reduce our need to always get our way is to practice listening more and showing curiosity about others' perspectives. By engaging in open dialogue and truly considering other viewpoints, we allow space for negotiation and collaboration.

More (+) Being heard: A great way to feel more heard is to learn how to share healthier boundaries.

Behavior	What It Gets Them	More or Less	Take Action
Know-It-All	Validation and be 'right'	+	Speak up about your needs and opinions
Short fuse	Control/Getting their way	-	Practice active listening and curiosity
Control freak	Being heard	+	Set healthy boundaries to ensure your voice is heard

Now, here's where the real magic happens: When you start doing the things you identified in the final column of this exercise, the other person's annoying behavior from the first column won't bother you anymore.

In other words, when you (1) speak up more, (2) listen more, and (3) set better boundaries, the other person being a know-it-all, angry, control freak won't trigger you anymore.

The concept of projection tells us that their behavior was only a problem because it brought up an unhealed part of ourselves. It was this misalignment—not the other person—that caused the discomfort. By refocusing on your own growth and meeting your own needs, you effectively neutralize the impact of their behavior and eliminate the trigger.

Ta-da! Trigger neutralized!

When we can learn to see someone else's behavior as a mirror, it stops being a trigger and starts being a tool. Their actions become nothing more than neutral reflections that provide valuable insights into our own role in the relationship and the world at large.

By completing the chart in this activity, you can create a shift in perspective that allows you to focus on your own growth and needs, rather than getting caught up in another person's drama. This is how we turn the biggest jerks in our lives into powerful guides on our journey to establishing healthy boundaries.

Questions About This Process?

Feel free to watch my video that walks you through this chart by visiting the Free Resources section of my coaching website at: www.livelifeunbroken.com.

THE PROBLEM OF PROJECTION

CHAPTER EIGHT
The Art of Being Self-ish

"Daring to set boundaries is about having the courage to love ourselves, even when we risk disappointing others." - Brené Brown

If you're anything like me, once you start recognizing just how much you have been ignoring *Who You Are* and you finally begin to focus on yourself a bit more, that's when those annoying little voices in your head start piping up, calling this newfound self-awareness the dreaded "S" word: Selfish.

So, let's talk about this.

The word *selfish* often gets a bad rap and can stir up some pretty strong emotions in people. In fact, many of us spend our entire lives doing everything we can to avoid being labeled as selfish. We bend over backward trying to please everyone around us only to find ourselves feeling burned out and completely overwhelmed.

So, how do we bring more balance? Let's start by re-examining the word *selfish*.

What It Means to Be Self-ish

If you break it down linguistically, the word *selfish* is made up of two parts: the word *Self* followed by the suffix *-ish*.

The word *Self* is easy as it's what we've been talking about for a few chapters now. Your *Self* refers to your essential, unique identity; the Core Essence of *Who You Are* that goes beyond your labels, roles and social masks and encompasses all aspects of you on all layers of reality—physical, mental, emotional and energetic. It includes your body, thoughts, feelings, consciousness, and all the other characteristics that make you, well, *You*.

Now, let's look at the suffix *-ish*.

If you were to think back to your grade school grammar days, when you first learned about suffixes, you might recall that a suffix is a linguistic element that you add to the end of a word to change its meaning or grammatical properties. It's like adding an accessory to an outfit. Just like a hat or scarf can change the entire look and feel of what you're wearing, a suffix can change the entire meaning of a word.

For example, take the word *happy*. Adding the suffix *-ness* transforms it into *happiness,* changing it from an adjective to a noun. Similarly, adding *-ly* to the word *quick* changes it to *quickly*, turning it into an adverb that describes how something is done.

Now, the suffix *-ish* is particularly interesting because it introduces a sense of approximation or flexibility to the word it accompanies. It's a way of saying that something is somewhat like the original word, but not completely.

For example, if I were to describe my neighbor as tall-*ish*, you would understand that I mean they are somewhat tall, but not really tall. They may have some characteristics of being tall, but maybe not enough to be outright classified as *tall*. Similarly, if I say my shirt is red-*ish*, you can understand that it's mainly red but not entirely. While it might have an overall red hue, there are other colors mixed in, making it not purely red.

HOW TO SET BOUNDARIES WITHOUT FEELING LIKE A D*CK

The suffix -*ish* helps convey that something has some qualities of the original word but not entirely, allowing for the communication of nuances and degrees. It softens the absoluteness of a word, making it less rigid and more adaptable.

In this context, when we talk about being Self-*ish*, we're actually referring to the idea of prioritizing ourselves—but not in an absolute way; it's about putting ourselves first while still caring about the needs and well-being of others. When understood through this lens, the idea of being Self-*ish* is actually a wonderful thing! It means you know how to take care of yourself and get your needs met, but not to the exclusion of, or at the expense of, other people. It is this balanced approach that allows us to be compassionate without having to resort to being 'Nice.'

And isn't that why you're here?

Being Self-*ish*, it turns out, is the goal. In fact, making yourself a priority without ignoring or dismissing other people is the entire point of having healthy boundaries in the first place. This is what gives you the energy to help others without losing yourself in the process.

Not only is this healthy, it's downright essential.

A few years ago, a man named Tom came to one of my healing retreats looking for something different. As an IT professional, Tom thrived on logic and order, but the increasing demands of his job and the sudden loss of his father had begun to take a toll. He was feeling burned out, and his patience at home was beginning to dwindle. While Tom wanted to be there for his wife and their two children, he often felt too exhausted to engage meaningfully. His wife, who had noticed the changes in Tom, suggested that he take some time off to attend a retreat and recharge. While he initially resisted, insisting he couldn't take time off work or step away from family responsibilities, his wife persisted, and Tom eventually agreed.

When Tom first arrived at the retreat, he was clearly outside his comfort zone. During the opening circle, he shared that he felt overwhelmed by all the things he had to do at home and at the office, and he felt guilty for leaving his wife to manage the kids alone. He felt like he was abandoning his family.

As he settled into the rhythm of the retreat, something began to shift. Away from all the daily demands, Tom started to unwind. The tranquil environment, combined with the supportive space and focus on emotional healing, began to have an effect, and for the first time in years, Tom said his mind began to relax. He started to smile and laugh and was engaging more meaningfully with the group.

By the end of the retreat, Tom reported that he felt rejuvenated. Away from the stress and responsibilities of daily life, he rediscovered parts of himself he had long forgotten existed and returned home with a renewed sense of purpose. This newfound self-awareness allowed him to be more present and engaged with his kids, more supportive of his wife, and even more productive at work. In fact, he later reported that he got a promotion!

Tom's story is the perfect example of what it means to be "Self-ish." By prioritizing his own well-being and taking time away to recharge, Tom wasn't neglecting his family's needs. Instead, he was ensuring that he was in the best state to take care of them.

This is the essence of being "Self-ish."

By taking time to care for ourselves, we can better serve those we love. And that is the most powerful boundary of all.

So, if the goal is to be Self-ish, the big question still remains: how do you start? You start by learning how to source your own energy.

Sourcing Your Energy

Every day, we expend an enormous amount of energy on work, relationships, family, kids, and countless other tasks like writing emails, cooking dinner, and running errands. Honestly, just the simple act of being a human can be draining some days! These mundane, everyday activities slowly chip away at our energy reserves and, if we're not careful, we can end up with nothing left for ourselves at the end of the day.

Sound familiar?

Most of us are taught that when we are feeling drained or overwhelmed, we should turn to our friends or family to lift our spirits. We say things like, "My kids are my everything; they give me all the love and energy I need," or "My friends always know just how to cheer me up." While this sounds wonderful, it raises a really important question: if being around them recharges you, what do you suppose is happening to their energy?

Hmmm...

Growing up, I had a friend who turned every hangout into a marathon venting session about her boss and her mother. As soon as we'd sit down, she'd dive into the latest drama, recounting every last detail while I sat there feeling more and more tired. She would leave our conversations feeling better, having gotten everything off her chest, while I'd walk away feeling completely exhausted and drained.

Eventually, I stopped wanting to hang out with her and our friendship fizzled out.

We all have that one person in our life who uses us as their emotional crutch, and we all know how it feels to be on the receiving end of their constant demands for support. It's exhausting, and it can create a real barrier to authentic connection. Similarly, when we constantly rely on others to recharge us and take care of our emotional needs, we can unintentionally drain their emotional energy and create an imbalance where one person feels like they're always giving, and the other is always taking.

Most of us do this without even realizing it because we have been taught that this is what relationships are supposed to be: "I complete you, you complete me, and together we are whole." While this idea might sound idyllic in movies and fairy tales, in reality, it can lead to unhealthy power dynamics and emotional codependency.

More on that later.

The truth is, when you rely on others to meet your emotional needs, you inadvertently place a heavy burden on them, which can leave them feeling depleted and overwhelmed, even if they don't realize why. Over time, instead of fostering mutual support and growth, the relationship can turn into a battleground for emotional survival.

Yikes.

To break free from this cycle, it's important to learn how to source your own energy by engaging in activities that nurture and replenish your emotional needs independently—without relying on other people. This requires you to learn how to tap into the infinite energy of Love.

The Power of Love

You may have heard love referred to as the underlying energy and vibration of the universe. While you might be tempted to roll your eyes, it has been scientifically proven that love is more than just a feeling; it is a complex human experience that profoundly influences and shapes our emotional, psychological and physiological development. Research has shown that the human heart emits an electromagnetic field that can be measured several feet away from the body.[11] The heart's electromagnetic field is not only the strongest rhythmic field produced by the human body, but it also plays a key role in influencing our emotional and physiological states.

According to the HeartMath Institute, a research and education organization dedicated to the study of the heart-brain connection, positive emotions, such as love, create smooth, synchronized patterns in our heart rhythms, a state they call *heart coherence*.[12] When we're in this state, not only do we feel better emotionally, but we also think more clearly, feel less stressed, and enjoy better overall health.

Numerous studies have also highlighted the profound impact of love on our early development. Research by Bowlby and Ainsworth on attachment theory emphasizes that early emotional bonds and love are crucial for psychological stability,[13] while studies on children raised in Romanian orphanages revealed extreme developmental delays due to neglect and lack of love.[14]

Love, it turns out, is for humans what sunlight is for plants. Just as plants reach for the sun to thrive, we require love to flourish. Everything we know about love shows that its absence can lead to devastating consequences, including attachment disorders, cognitive delays, poor physical health, and social and behavioral issues.

Therefore, love is not a luxury but a fundamental human need that is essential for our survival. The question is, how do we tap into this powerful energy of love without relying on other people?

It's actually quite simple: just do things you love.

That's it.

Lighting Up Your Soul

Think about those moments when you felt truly happy and alive—whether you were sipping your favorite gourmet latte, taking your dog for a long hike, or blasting your favorite tunes. These simple, everyday activities might seem ordinary, but they're actually so much more. Every time you engage in doing something that you love, these small acts become powerful conduits that connect you to a deeper energy of love.

We tend to think that love can only come from our relationships with others, but there's so much more to it than that. In fact, if you're only relying on friends and family to feel loved, you're missing out on a big piece of the puzzle. When we take time to do things that genuinely make us happy, we tap into the energy of love in a way that has the power to recharge and replenish us—without the risk of draining others. More importantly, it allows us to bring more love and positivity into our relationships by showing up already recharged and full. This is an important part of boundary-setting that many of us miss.

Learning to manage your energy by tapping into the energy of love isn't some hippy-dippy nonsense; it's a critical skill that is essential for establishing healthy boundaries.

When you choose to recharge yourself from this deeper source of love, you can stop relying on others to fill your emotional tank and instead, become a positive force, both for yourself and those around you. This makes sharing and maintaining your boundaries easier because you're coming from a place of strength and self-reliance, rather than need, emptiness, or lack.

THE ART OF BEING SELF-ISH

This is how we turn our boundaries into a powerful force of change and healing in our world.

This is the magic of boundaries.

CHAPTER EIGHT ACTIVITY
What Lights Up Your Soul

When life feels overwhelming and you're running on empty, setting boundaries will feel like an impossible task. That's why, before you even think about sharing your boundaries or expressing your needs with others, it's essential to recharge yourself first.

In this activity, you'll focus on discovering what truly lights up your soul by exploring those activities that make you lose track of time and bring a genuine smile to your face.

Your goal is to create a list of 30 activities that Light Up Your Soul.

I know, I know—I can almost hear your brain freaking out. But trust me, you can do this. When I first asked myself this question, I, too, struggled with where to even begin. While it was easy for me to list what made others happy, figuring out what brought me joy was a challenge.

Here's the good news: this is easier than you think. In fact, just setting the intention to discover what lights up your soul is a really great start. This small shift in mindset can help you begin to become more aware of and responsible for your own energy. And that's a pretty big deal, don't you think?

Simply start by asking yourself, "What lights up my soul?" as often as you can remember. The more you ask, the more you'll start to notice the little things that genuinely bring you joy. It could be a hobby from your childhood, a new activity that piques your interest, or even a simple walk with your dog. By focusing on this question, you create a new boundary with yourself and the universe, one that prioritizes your well-being and embraces being Self-*ish* in the most empowered way possible.

Remember, there are only two criteria for this:

(1) It must genuinely bring a smile to your face. If your reaction is, "Well, I guess *maybe* this makes me happy," it probably doesn't Light Up Your Soul.

(2) It cannot rely on another person—kids, partners, and friends are not allowed on this list. You need to fill up your own energy so that when you show up for your loved ones, you are full, not empty and needy.

To help you explore this more deeply, grab a notebook or your journal, a pen, and find a quiet, comfortable space where you won't be disturbed. Take a few deep breaths and get settled.

Step 1: Reflect on Your Past

Think back to your childhood. What activities did you absolutely love? Climbing trees, drawing with crayons, playing make-believe? Jot down anything that made you feel alive and joyful, no matter how small or silly it might seem.

These early passions can hold clues to what truly lights up your soul, even if you haven't revisited them in years.

Next, think about your teenage years and early adulthood. What hobbies or interests did you have that made you lose track of time? Maybe it was playing a sport, writing poetry, or exploring the outdoors. Write these down too.

Oftentimes, the interests we had during these stages reflect deeper parts of ourselves that long to be rediscovered.

Step 2: Explore Your Present

Now let's focus on your current life. What activities, even if they're rare, bring you genuine happiness and satisfaction? Think about recent moments when you felt truly happy and fulfilled. Maybe it was reading a great book, trying a new recipe, or spending time outdoors. Write down anything that comes to mind, no matter how small it might seem.

If you're stuck, ask yourself: When was the last time I felt really excited or enthusiastic about something? What was I doing? Write down whatever pops up, even if you're not sure yet if it belongs on your list.

HOW TO SET BOUNDARIES WITHOUT FEELING LIKE A D*CK

Step 3: Dream About Your Future

Now, imagine your ideal day. What activities would it include? If you had unlimited time and resources, what would you do? Maybe it's enjoying a leisurely breakfast, hiking in nature, or spending the afternoon painting. Write down these dream activities.

Finally, think about any new hobbies or skills you've always wanted to try but haven't yet. Perhaps it's learning to play the guitar, baking elaborate cakes, or taking a road trip to explore new places. List these potential activities too.

If you need more ideas, feel free to explore the following various categories of activities. As you go through them, see if anything else comes to mind and add those to your list.

Physical Activities: Going to the gym, doing a home workout, or joining a fitness class. Taking a dance class, dancing at home, or going out dancing with friends. Exploring local trails, visiting national parks, or hiking in the mountains. Practicing yoga at a studio, at home with online videos, or in a park. Jogging in your neighborhood, running in a park, or training for a marathon. Swimming at a local pool, at the beach, or in a lake. Biking around your city, taking a spin class, or mountain biking. Joining a local sports league, playing tennis, or shooting hoops. Taking a karate, judo, or kickboxing class. Indoor rock climbing at a gym or outdoor climbing on natural rock formations. Hula hoop dancing.

Creative Pursuits: Working with watercolors, oils, or acrylics, or taking a painting class. Journaling, writing poetry, working on a novel, or starting a blog. Making handmade cards, jewelry, or decorations. Creating clothes, accessories, or home decor items. Designing and making quilts for yourself or as gifts. Knitting and needlepoint. Cross stitching. Taking photos around your neighborhood, setting up photo shoots, or traveling for photography. Sketching, illustrating, or creating digital art. Collecting and arranging photos and memorabilia into creative layouts. Taking a pottery class, working with clay at home, or visiting a pottery studio. Learning an instrument, composing music, or playing in a band. Singing, karaoke, joining a choir or barbershop quartet.

Learning and Growth: Enjoying novels, non-fiction books, or magazines. Enrolling in online classes, attending workshops, or taking night classes at a local college. Picking up a new language, learning to code, or mastering a new craft. Finding podcasts on topics that interest you, such as history, science, or personal development. Exploring documentaries on various subjects, from nature to politics. Participating in webinars, conferences, or live events. Giving your time to a cause you care about and learning from the experience. Becoming a member of a book club, hobby group, or professional organization. Sharing your knowledge and experience with others. Practicing meditation, mindfulness exercises, or attending retreats.

Relaxation and Pampering: Enjoying a hot bath with candles, bath salts, and relaxing music. Visiting a nail salon or doing a manicure/pedicure at home. Setting aside time for daily meditation or using guided meditation apps. Booking a professional massage or using a massage chair. Creating a relaxing playlist or discovering new music. Curling up with a good book in a cozy spot. Taking short, refreshing naps during the day. Using essential oils and diffusers to create a calming atmosphere. Binge-watching a favorite series or watching comforting movies. Taking a break to savor a hot beverage.

Nature and Outdoors: Planting flowers, vegetables, or creating a herb garden. Taking leisurely strolls in local parks or nature reserves. Spending weekends camping in the wilderness or at a campground. Observing and identifying birds in your area. Packing a picnic and enjoying a meal outdoors with friends or family. Going fishing at a local lake, river, or ocean. Watching the night sky and identifying constellations. Walking along the beach and collecting shells or rocks. Golfing or visiting a driving range. Cycling on nature trails or through scenic areas. Capturing the beauty of landscapes, plants, and wildlife with your camera. Sitting around a campfire.

Step 4: Compile Your List

Once you've explored all the perspectives and options, it's time to compile your master list. Take all the ideas you've written down and refine them, removing anything that doesn't belong and adding any new ideas that come up. Your goal is to create a list of 30 activities you can refer to when life gets overwhelming.

HOW TO SET BOUNDARIES WITHOUT FEELING LIKE A D*CK

If you're still struggling to reach 30, that's okay. Be patient with yourself and allow your list to grow over time. Exploring these questions can create profound ripples of change, and you may discover more sources of joy than you initially realized. Keep asking, and keep adding!

Need even more inspiration? Here are some ideas inspired by my own list to help to get those creative juices flowing:

- Enjoy a cup of your favorite tea or coffee.
- Take a few minutes to watch the sunrise or sunset.
- Listen to your favorite song or playlist.
- Go for a brisk walk and enjoy the fresh air.
- Cuddle with your pet or a stuffed animal.
- Light a scented candle or use essential oils.
- Read a few pages of a good book.
- Warm up a blanket in the dryer and wrap yourself in it.
- Creative or journal writing.
- Indulge in a piece of your favorite chocolate or treat.
- Play a card or board game.
- Stretch or do a quick yoga pose.
- Practice deep breathing or a short meditation.
- Look at photos that make you happy.
- Watch a funny video or stand-up comedy clip.
- Make silly faces at yourself in the mirror (yes, I actually do this).
- Let loose a string of raunchy swear words (this is a personal favorite of mine!)
- Appreciate a beautiful flower or plant.
- Give yourself a mini hand or foot massage.

- Draw or doodle for a few minutes.
- Look up at the sky and notice the clouds or stars.
- Dance to a favorite song.
- Savor a piece of fruit.
- Daydream about something you love.
- Take a short nap.
- Enjoy your favorite fancy cocktail.
- Watch birds or other wildlife.
- Listen to the sound of rain or nature sounds.
- Treat yourself to a piece of fancy cheese or a special snack.
- People-watch in a park or busy area.
- Enjoy a hot shower or bath with your favorite bath products.
- Savor a warm cup of soup or hot cocoa.
- Create a small piece of art, like a quick sketch or craft project.
- Practice mindfulness, focusing on the present.
- Put on a cozy sweater or blanket.
- Wear funky socks or fun earrings
- Watch a few minutes of a nature documentary or your favorite TV show.
- Write a kind note to yourself or someone else.
- Rearrange a small space in your home to make it feel fresh.
- Appreciate a beautiful piece of art or photography.

Some Helpful Tips

Most of us spend so little time paying attention to what truly lights us up that, at first, reconnecting with our own energy can feel unfamiliar and even a little strange. The good news is once you get the hang of it, it becomes much easier.

HOW TO SET BOUNDARIES WITHOUT FEELING LIKE A D*CK

To help you along, here are some tips to help you realign to your desires.

(1) No Should Zone:

Sourcing your own energy means doing things that genuinely bring a smile to your face—which means no "shoulds" are allowed on your list. If something doesn't truly make you happy, it doesn't count toward replenishing your energy.

For example, a few years ago, my good friend treated me to a one-hour massage at an exclusive spa. She lived for her monthly massages, and every time she talked about her upcoming spa day, her eyes would light up. The place she sent me to was amazing—soothing music, scented candles, the whole works. While I appreciated the thought and my muscles certainly felt looser afterward, it didn't light me up the same way it did for her. To be honest, lying half-naked on a table making small talk with a stranger while they touch me is not my idea of a good time. So, while the massage lit up my friend's soul and brought her joy, my experience was more about doing something good for my body rather than something I loved.

There's a big difference between doing things that are good for you and doing things that truly Light Up Your Soul. As adults, we often need to engage in activities that maintain our health and well-being, like brushing our teeth, cleaning the house, and exercising regularly.

While these tasks are essential for keeping us healthy and functioning, they don't necessarily bring us any pleasure. For instance, having a clean house makes me feel happy, but does cleaning my house light up my soul? Definitely not.

Sourcing energy involves intentionally doing things that make you feel alive and genuinely happy. While it's important to take care of your basic needs, it's equally important to engage in activities that bring you pure joy. Being Self-*ish* and sourcing your own energy means making time for both: taking care of yourself and embracing the things that truly light you up.

(2) Make It Suck Less:

I get that some days are tough, and sometimes finding the time to Light Up Your Soul may be the last thing on your mind. I mean, some days we barely have time for the 'shoulds,' let alone for doing things that light us up, right?

And isn't that kind of the problem?

Years ago, I worked as a practice manager in a very busy veterinary hospital. While the thought of playing with cute puppies and kittens might sound appealing, the reality often involved dealing with severely injured, abused, or neglected animals. The high-stress environment was emotionally taxing, and I often needed to find ways to bring a little levity into my day.

This is when I discovered the joy of silly socks.

Long before it was trendy, I was sporting loud and crazy socks—the weirder, the better. My theory was simple: a tough day filled with challenging cases and losing patients was rough, but doing it all while wearing bright daffodils on my feet made it just a tiny bit easier to handle. It didn't make the hard days good, but it did make them suck a little less. And sometimes, that's enough.

These small acts of joy, no matter how miniscule, can help us cope with the emotional toll of being a human. While wearing my playful socks certainly didn't change the challenging situations, it was a tiny bit of self-care—a small sourcing of energy—that made a significant difference.

(3) Weave It In:

We may not always be able drop everything to do something we love, but we can learn to weave soul-boosting activities into our daily routine.

Think about those energy-draining tasks like paying bills or driving the kids around. Instead of dreading them, ask yourself, "How can I infuse a bit of joy into this moment?" Maybe you light a candle and sip your favorite tea while handling your finances, or roll down the windows and blast your favorite music while on the road.

These small changes can transform mundane tasks into moments of pleasure, making your day a bit brighter and less stressful.

For instance, being a small business owner means I have to deal with the drudgery of filing my taxes regularly—a task that I mostly dread because it's so boring. To help stop it from being an energy drain, I have learned to layer in some things that bring me joy. For example, I often make myself a fancy chai latte and burn my favorite incense while I do my bookkeeping. I will also wear my fuzziest socks and play relaxing piano jazz music in the background to create a nice little atmosphere for myself.

Learning to source your energy means finding creative ways to add joy to the everyday chores on your to-do list. Maybe you turn folding laundry into a mini karaoke party or maybe you listen to your favorite podcast while cooking dinner. Even the smallest changes, like using a scented hand lotion or lighting your favorite candle, can make a big difference to how you feel.

And the more you're filled with the energy of love, the easier it is to speak up and share your boundaries.

THE ART OF BEING SELF-ISH

CHAPTER NINE
Where You End and Others Begin

"Good fences make good neighbors." - Robert Frost

Now that you have a better understanding of *Who You Are* and how to source your energy so you can show up whole and grounded in your relationships, it's finally time to dive into the nuts and bolts of setting boundaries. And since so many of us get this wrong, I want to begin by first clarifying what boundaries are <u>not</u>.

Boundaries are not just about saying 'No,' although that can be a part of it. While it is true that 'No' is a complete sentence, simply saying 'No' doesn't do anything to ensure your needs are being acknowledged or met—which is kind of the whole point of speaking up in the first place.

Boundaries are not about unloading a laundry list of grievances onto another person, or dictating what they should or shouldn't do. While it may seem helpful to voice disappointment and offer constructive criticism, this approach often backfires, putting others on the defensive and obscuring the message of your boundary.

Boundaries are also not a platform for sharing your feelings. While, yes, expressing your emotions is a vital part of healthy communication, sharing your feelings is not the same thing as sharing a boundary.

Finally, boundaries are not a tool to get someone else to change their behavior. The reality is, people are allowed to be obnoxious, ignorant, know-it-all jackasses, and nothing you say or do can ever truly change that. If you only share what you want in the sole hopes of getting the other person to change, that's not a healthy boundary. In fact, setting boundaries with the expectation that the other person will change is a form of covert manipulation that can undermine connection and completely break trust.

More on this is a moment.

So, if boundaries aren't about saying '*No*,' venting your feelings, or telling someone else what they need to do differently—what are they about?

Sharing What You Want

At their core, boundaries are about understanding your own wants, needs, and desires, and then expressing them in a way that empowers both you and the other person; they are about building a bridge that connects you to others—honoring both *Who You Are* and *Who They Are* as well. Boundaries are what create a safe space where everyone involved can openly share their thoughts and feelings, without fear of rejection or negative repercussions; they are what allow collaboration and authentic connection to thrive.

A few years ago, my neighbor's sister, Caroline, was telling me about a tricky situation she was in with her good friend, Sarah. They were very close, and for many years had been getting together regularly to share everything from daily frustrations to big dreams. However, Caroline was beginning to feel overwhelmed by their constant interactions. Sarah would often call late at night, needing to vent about her day, and while Caroline valued their friendship, she started feeling drained and reluctant to answer the phone when she saw Sarah's name pop up on her screen. Eventually, Caroline realized she needed to speak up and set a boundary, but was nervous about how Sarah would react. She didn't want Sarah to think she was pushing her away or that she didn't care.

One evening, after a particularly exhausting day, she decided it was time to say something. Caroline began by expressing how much she valued their friendship, and how important Sarah was to her.

Then, she compassionately expressed her boundary.

"Sarah," she said, "I love our late-night chats, and I love hearing all about what is going on in your life, and I would love if we could have our calls a little earlier in the evening." Caroline heard a slight hesitation, but then Sarah responded, "Oh sure – of course! Actually, that would work better for me as well!"

From that moment on, they adjusted their routine and this conversation ultimately strengthened their friendship. By setting a boundary and ensuring her needs were being met, Caroline created a healthier space for both of them. It allowed her to recharge and be more present when they did connect, and it gave Sarah the opportunity to understand and respect Caroline's needs. This made Sarah feel trusted as well and it deepened their bond.

This is the goal of healthy boundaries.

Contrary to popular belief, boundaries aren't about shutting people out or being cold, rude or aggressive. They're not about dumping all your frustrations and emotions on other people either. Instead, boundaries are about creating a space that honors the needs of everyone involved and—when done correctly—they are what allow you to express your desires without the burden of expecting the other person to do anything about it.

Let's go a little deeper, shall we?

Where You Are and Where You Are Not

When I talk about boundaries, I am referring to having an understanding of your personal limits and recognizing what you can and cannot control.

Think of it like this: Imagine your personal space as a large circle. Inside this circle are all your wants, needs, thoughts, feelings, opinions, values, and everything else that makes up the entirety of *Who You Are*. Within this circle, you have complete power and authority because everything inside is within your sphere of influence.

Now, imagine that the other people in your life also have their own circles, each containing their unique wants, needs, thoughts, feelings, opinions, values, and everything else that makes up the entirety of *Who They Are*.

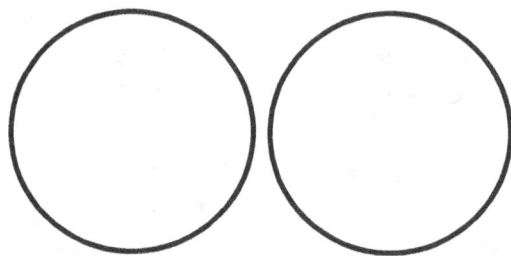

Because the contents of their circles are outside of yours, they are completely beyond your control. This means that no matter how much you want to help or change someone else, you cannot dictate what happens inside their circle. This lack of control can be incredibly frustrating because, as humans, we naturally crave certainty, and when we can't manage a situation, we feel powerless. We then believe it is our job to express our frustration and sense of powerlessness to the other person in the hope that they'll do something about it. After all, if they knew how much their behavior was affecting us, surely they would change, right?

But here's the uncomfortable truth: it's not someone else's job to change just to make you comfortable.

Someone else's actions and reactions are entirely within their circle and, therefore, completely outside your control. In fact, when we try to make ourselves responsible for how others feel and behave, we give away our power to change our own lives. This is what it means to *'give away your power'*—having poor boundaries, making ourselves responsible for things we can't control, and relinquishing the power to change what we actually can.

The Vesica Piscis

Let's do a quick recap: your circle is yours, and it holds all of your wants, needs, desires, thoughts, opinions, beliefs, and everything else that makes up *Who You Are*. The circles of other people, similarly, hold all their unique wants, needs, desires, thoughts, opinions, beliefs, and everything else that makes them *Who They Are*. But what happens when we want to enter into a relationship with another person? What happens when we want to let someone actually get to know us?

When we connect with another person—whether in a romantic partnership, a friendship, a work relationship, or any other type of connection—our circles inevitably move close enough to create a shared space where they begin to overlap. This overlapped area is a space where both you and the other person have some measure of control—but not total control. This space is neither entirely yours nor theirs, making it a shared space for negotiation and collaboration; a space where something new can be born.

In sacred geometry, the metaphysical study of shapes and their deeper meanings, the shape created by two partially overlapping circles is known as the *Vesica Piscis,* which is formed when each circle's center lies on the circumference of the other.

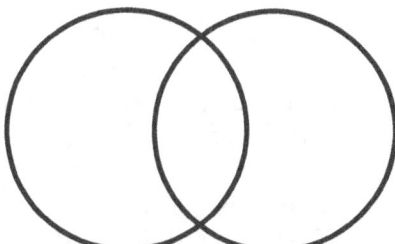

This creates a new shape in the middle that resembles an elongated fish, an almond, or a sideways eye. Sometimes called *mandorla* in Italian, this geometric figure is often depicted in Christian art as an almond-shaped aura or halo that typically surrounds Christ or the Virgin Mary. It symbolizes the union of two worlds—the Holy Trinity and the birthplace of creation—and represents a space where something entirely new can emerge.[15] While the Vesica Piscis isn't typically associated with boundaries, I, personally, find it to be a beautiful metaphor for understanding the interaction between our circle and those of others.

When we move towards another person's circle to develop a relationship—whether it's a friendship, a romantic relationship, or any other type of connection—we inevitably create a shared space that generates the Vesica Piscis with our combined circles. In this shared space, we are called upon to become more than *Who We Are* on our own. Here, we have the ability to create something greater than what we could accomplish individually—and that's a beautiful thing. It is through this connection and blending of our circle with others' that we grow, learn, and evolve as individuals.

It is also where boundaries become critical.

The Passive-Aggressive Cycle

Earlier, I mentioned that expecting someone else to change their behavior when you set boundaries is a recipe for disaster and often triggers a *passive-aggressive* cycle.

What do I mean by that?

Let's go back to your circle for a moment.

Without healthy boundaries, when we enter into a relationship—whether it's romantic, platonic, or otherwise—we can easily become confused about what space is ours (physically, mentally, emotionally, and energetically) and what belongs to the other person. As a result, we might find ourselves swinging between two extremes: either getting so wrapped up in the other person's circle that we neglect our own needs, or shutting them out entirely, leaving us feeling isolated and unwanted.

When we are entirely focused on another person's circle—trying to anticipate and fulfill their needs, manage their emotions, and make them happy—we are on the passive side of the cycle. In this state, our own circle becomes our blind spot, leaving our wants and needs mostly unacknowledged and unmet. When we do this, we unintentionally reject and abandon ourselves in order to avoid conflict and keep the peace; we choose being 'Nice' at the expense of our own sense of self and identity.

Oops.

In this passive state, we might find ourselves saying 'Yes' to things we dislike, or staying silent when we're actually upset, all to avoid conflict and keep the other person happy with us. On the surface, it might seem like everything is running smoothly—after all, there's no real conflict—but underneath, resentment and frustration are quietly building.

For example, imagine you have a teenage daughter who wants to attend a late-night party. You worry that if you say no, she'll just sneak out anyway, and you don't want to be seen as the "uncool" parent or risk her being angry with you. So, despite your concerns, you say yes, even though deep down you're feeling anxious and upset. In doing so, you've ignored your own boundaries and neglected your need for peace of mind.

Or, let's say you're in a brand-new relationship and start feeling insecure, wondering whether the other person is being truthful with you. Instead of speaking up and sharing your concerns—fearing it might cause discomfort—you stay quiet and pretend everything is fine. In this case, you have ignored your own need for clarity and reassurance. Over time, this chronic self-neglect can erode your sense of self and harm your closest relationships. You may start to believe that the only way to keep the peace is to go against your better judgment or just stay silent.

Eventually, this will lead to feelings of resentment and anxiety—which you'll also have to suppress in the name of maintaining peace.

For many people, they will spend their entire lives stuck on the passive side of the cycle, perpetually being 'Nice', ignoring their own needs, and neglecting the unique aspects of themselves that make them *Who They Are*. For others, there inevitably comes a point when they start thinking, "Hey, wait a minute – what about me, dammit?" Eventually, being 'Nice' loses its appeal and we begin to feel overwhelmed and exhausted from constantly trying to carry everyone else's burdens.

And that's when the anger sets in.

At this point, we flip to the aggressive side of the cycle, thinking, "Screw this—I'm tired of doing what everyone else wants. What about me?" We may get loud, frustrated, and lash out, venting our complaints to anyone who will listen. Or we might convince ourselves that we "don't care," try to swallow our anger, and put on a happy face, only to have it seep out anyway.

For instance, we might snap and yell, "I'm tired of no one listening to what I have to say," or we might make more subtle comments like, "I would hate to find out I was being lied to," hoping the other person will pick up on our cryptic messages and change their behavior.

These reactions are attempts to release the pent-up frustration and resentment we've been holding on to while being passive and 'Nice.' The problem is that while speaking up this way might feel empowering, confrontation is no fun and being aggressive doesn't actually improve our lives. In fact, it often leads to negative consequences, such as pushing others away, eroding intimacy and trust, or creating unnecessary drama and conflict.

Eventually, the guilt and remorse will start to creep in because we know these behaviors don't truly reflect *Who We Are*, and we don't like ourselves when we're being angry all the time. We get exhausted from the constant battles and from the effort of having to guard the emotional walls we've built around ourselves. In response, we might promise ourselves to just smile and stay silent, quietly slipping back into passive mode, and once again focusing on pleasing others just to keep the peace. We return to pushing our own needs aside in the hope of feeling liked, loved, and accepted.

As you can imagine, constantly swinging back and forth between focusing on your own needs and focusing on others creates a rollercoaster of emotions that can lead to a lot of instability in close relationships. When others don't know which version of you will show up—*'Nice'* or aggressive—the lack of consistency breaks trust.

For some, this toxic cycle can persist for years, affecting relationships with partners, kids, parents, family, coworkers, and friends. Without healthy boundaries, we risk becoming trapped in these toxic cycles, which can eventually lead to emotional co-dependency. What do I mean by that?

Let's revisit your circle.

The Trap of Emotional Co-Dependency

As you now know, your circle includes all your wants, needs, beliefs, desires, thoughts, opinions, and values. Similarly, other people's circles contain theirs. Ideally, there's just enough overlap to create the Vesica Piscis—a space where we can collaborate and create something new together, while still maintaining the integrity of our individual circles.

But what happens when the circles overlap a little too much?

When both people become overly focused on each other, their circles will almost completely overlap. This is the essence of emotional co-dependency—a state where personal boundaries blur and individuality is sacrificed, creating an unhealthy dynamic where each person's sense of self is heavily reliant on the other.

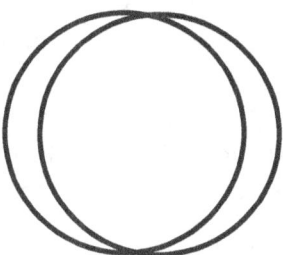

Co-dependency is an unhealthy and dysfunctional way of relating to others, characterized by a complete and total lack of healthy boundaries. In a co-dependent relationship, whether romantic, platonic, professional, or otherwise, one or both individuals rely heavily on the other to meet most of their emotional needs, self-worth, and sense of identity, believing they need the other person to feel whole, worthy, and enough.

This reliance can create an unhealthy dynamic where each person's identity becomes so entangled with the other's that maintaining individuality and a strong sense of self becomes nearly impossible. In essence, the line between *Who We Are* and *Who They Are* becomes blurry, making it difficult for each person to distinguish their own needs and emotions from those of the other.

Back in university, I had a friend named Melanie who always seemed to be in a relationship. Melanie was kind and caring but often got so absorbed in her boyfriend's life that her own needs and desires were sidelined. Melanie would adopt her boyfriend's hobbies, interests, and even his opinions and political views. If we had plans but her boyfriend called, she would cancel and drop everything to be with him, believing that this was what it meant to be in love. When her boyfriend was happy, Melanie felt happy. When he was upset, she felt responsible for fixing it and making him feel better. This emotional co-dependency created an unhealthy dynamic where Melanie's happiness and sense of self-worth hinged entirely on her boyfriend's mood and approval.

Over time, this imbalance inevitably led to explosive fights and instability, causing their relationship to crumble. Sadly, Melanie would then repeat this cycle with the next boyfriend, perpetuating the same unhealthy patterns and never fully addressing her own part in the problem.

When we lose our sense of self because we're so busy managing and trying to control things in someone else's circle, our circle inevitably gets neglected. Worse, when we live inside someone else's circle, we have zero control or power to change anything.

No wonder it feels so awful.

The harsh truth is, if you've been people-pleasing, ignoring your boundaries, and being '*Nice*' to keep the peace and avoid conflict, you're actually contributing to the problem.

By neglecting your own needs and boundaries, you unintentionally create an environment where genuine connection, respect, and trust cannot flourish.

Uh-oh.

HOW TO SET BOUNDARIES WITHOUT FEELING LIKE A D*CK

The Limits of Independence

On the flip side, many of us have been taught that maintaining complete and total independence in our relationships—whether it's romantic, professional, or any other type of connection—is the ultimate goal. Society has glorified independence-based relationships for so long that it's often seen as the ideal. But, this can be just as unhealthy. In a state of complete independence, our circle, and the other person's circle, don't intersect at all; they remain entirely separate.

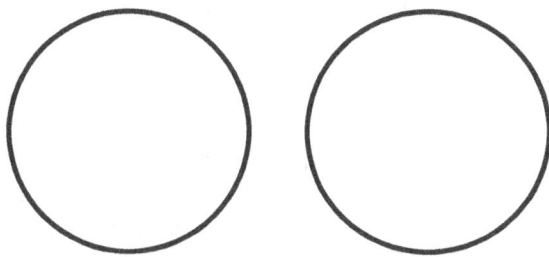

You might be thinking, "What's the big deal? Isn't maintaining independence a good thing—isn't that what we're supposed to do?" The problem is, when we keep our circle completely separate from everyone else, we risk feeling isolated and left out—like we're always on the outside looking in, never truly belonging. While the mindset of 'I don't need anyone, I'm fine on my own' might be celebrated as ideal, it can leave us feeling lonely, unfulfilled, and unwanted. Plus, it can get in the way of forming authentic and meaningful connections.

Let's say you're in a relationship where you never fully share your thoughts, emotions, or experiences with the other person out of fear of being judged or causing an argument. While, sure, you might avoid conflict and keep things smooth on the surface, you're also missing out on the deep, fulfilling connection that comes from being truly open with another person. When you hold back like this, it creates a barrier to genuine intimacy and understanding. Over time, this lack of vulnerability can lead to feelings of loneliness and disconnection, leaving both you and the other person feeling unfulfilled and the relationship lacking the depth and warmth it needs to thrive.

Back when I was working in veterinary hospitals, I worked with a nurse named Danny who took great pride in his independence. After being hurt badly in past relationships, he decided that strict boundaries and complete independence were the best ways to protect himself. In his marriage, he and his wife led very separate lives, with their own interests, friends, and routines.

Initially, this arrangement seemed ideal as there were no arguments about personal space or autonomy. Over time, however, Danny began to feel an indescribable sense of emptiness. Despite being physically together, they were emotionally distant, lacking the warmth and connection that come from shared experiences and mutual support. Eventually, they separated, attributing it to simply "growing apart."

When we don't allow our circle to overlap with those of our friends, family, and loved ones, it can lead to relationships that are unfulfilling. Just as co-dependency blurs the boundaries between individuals, complete independence can prevent the development of meaningful relationships. By keeping ourselves too distant, we may avoid the messiness of human interaction, but we also miss out on the support, intimacy, and mutual growth that healthy relationships provide.

So, what's the solution? How can we nurture close, vulnerable relationships without losing our identity or feeling like we have to act like a total dick just to be heard?

The answer, of course, is boundaries.

Boundaries are what allow you to find a healthy balance where your circle overlaps with someone else's just enough to create the Vesica Piscis—a shared space where you can explore *Who You Are* through the lens of the relationship. This is only possible with healthy boundaries and is the foundation for what is known as *interdependence*.

The Vesica Piscis of Interdependence

Interdependence is the healthiest way to relate to others because it allows you to maintain your individuality and self-sufficiency while recognizing that you can also rely on and support others. In an interdependent relationship, your circle and the other person's circle remain intact but share that overlapping space, creating the Vesica Piscis.

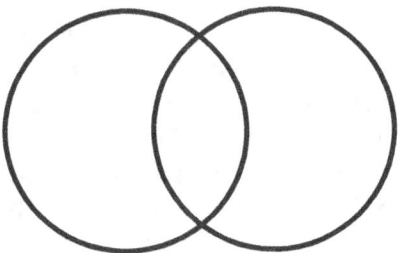

In this arrangement, you'll notice that a significant portion of your circle remains uniquely yours and is not part of the shared space. These are the individual aspects of *Who You Are*—your core values, beliefs, and personal standards—that you bring into the relationship without compromising. This dynamic allows you to uphold your identity while also being open to influence and growth.

A few years ago, my husband and I were invited to a BBQ at a friend's house. It was a large gathering, and the backyard was filled with a mix of friends, family, and kids of various ages. As the adults chatted, I noticed the kids began to form their own little social circles, each displaying different relational patterns.

First, I noticed Emily and Jack, cousins who always seemed to be glued to each other. Emily, the older one, took the lead in deciding what games to play and Jack followed obediently, never voicing his own preferences. When Emily suggested they play house, Jack immediately agreed, despite clearly looking more interested in the soccer game happening nearby. Their dynamic was one of complete reliance—Jack depended on Emily to make decisions for both of them, and Emily depended on Jack's compliance to feel wanted.

In stark contrast, there were the independent kids, like Lisa and Ben. Lisa preferred to play alone, setting up her own little picnic for her dolls far from the others. She seemed content but isolated, not interacting much with the other kids. Ben, on the other hand, was very assertive, often taking over group games. He decided the rules of hide-and-seek and expected everyone to follow them, showing little regard for the others' ideas. These kids demonstrated self-sufficiency, but their lack of collaboration and connection with others was pretty obvious.

Then there were the interdependent kids, a small group that included my friend's nephew, Sam, and his friends Mia and Jake. Watching them was fascinating. As someone who grew witnessing co-dependency and toxic relationship patterns, watching these kids connect with each other so effortlessly was an absolute delight. They took turns proposing different games, from tag to building a fort with the picnic blankets. Each child's idea was met with enthusiasm and they worked together seamlessly, each contributing and enjoying the process. When Sam suggested a scavenger hunt, Mia and Jake jumped in with their own ideas for clues and prizes. When there was a disagreement, they diplomatically talked it over and came up with a plan that everyone could get on board with. They showed a perfect balance of leading and following, respecting each other's input and making sure everyone was included.

This is the power of finding that sweet spot in our relationships where we can maintain our own identities while also embracing the strengths and ideas of others.

This is the power of boundaries.

A healthy, interdependent relationship is built on mutual trust and respect, and aims to create a balance of giving, and receiving, to ensure that everyone can maintain their autonomy and personal integrity, while also supporting and benefiting from one another. Just like those interdependent kids, the healthiest relationships are those where we can lead and follow, give and receive, and grow together—without losing ourselves in the process.

In the following chapters, I am going to outline exactly when, how, and what you can say to ensure that you're speaking up effectively, and in a way that feels good for both you and the other people in your life. As we continue forward, remember that your boundaries are unique to you. They reflect your understanding of *Who You Are*, and might differ from what your family, best friend, or boss might choose for themselves—and that's perfectly okay.

HOW TO SET BOUNDARIES WITHOUT FEELING LIKE A D*CK

At the end of the day, this is your life, and you get to create the standards and boundaries that define how you show up and express *Who You Are.*

WHERE YOU END AND OTHERS BEGIN

CHAPTER NINE ACTIVITY
Where Do You End and Others Begin?

Understanding your boundaries means being able to recognize where you end and where other people begin; it means identifying what you can control versus what you can't. This activity is designed to help you discover the edge of *Who You Are*, so you can clearly define your personal limits. By identifying this border, you can become more aware of your Core Needs, which will serve as the foundation for your new, healthy boundaries.

For this exercise, all you need is a pen, your journal or a notebook, and a few moments to yourself.

Step One: Identify Your Boundaries

Answer the following questions with at least 10 examples for each. I've included a few to get you started—feel free to use them as they are or as inspiration to come up with your own.

Q1. Fill in the blank: People may not _____

Examples: Go through my personal belongings, criticize me, make comments about my weight, take their anger out on me, humiliate me in front of others, tell off-color jokes in my company, invade my personal space.

Q2. Fill in the blank: I have a right to ask for _____

Example: Privacy, a new hairstyle from an old stylist, peace and quiet while getting a massage, help around the house, more information before making a purchase, quiet time to myself.

Q3. Fill in the blank: To protect my time and energy, it's okay to

Examples: Turn the ringer off my phone, take my time returning calls or emails, change my mind, bow out of a volunteer activity, cancel a commitment when I'm not feeling well, reserve a place in my home that is off-limits to others.

WHERE YOU END AND OTHERS BEGIN

Step Two: Identify Who You Are

Complete the following sentences to help you get super clear on exactly *Who You Are*. Aim for 3-5 examples for each.

Q1. Fill in the blank: I am _____

Examples: Kind, Smart, Fun, Loveable, Funny

Q2. Fill in the blank: I am not _____

Examples: Stupid, Silly, Irrelevant, Dumb

Q3. Fill in the blank: I want _____

Examples: Love, Money, Health, Pets in my life, Joy, Security

Q4. Fill in the blank: I do not want _____

Examples: Harsh words, Betrayal, Fear, Illness

Q5. Fill in the blank: I will _____

Examples: Take care of myself, Eat healthy, Take my supplements

Q6. Fill in the blank: I will not _____

Examples: Expect others to take care of me, Ignore my needs, Stay silent to please others

Okay, now for the final step.

Step Three: Identify your Core Needs

Once you've determined what is and isn't okay with you, it's time to dig a little deeper. In this step, you'll revisit your answers from Step One to uncover the core need behind each response. This will help you uncover what truly matters to you and reveal the deeper motivations that will shape your boundaries.

Let's go through some examples together so you can get a better understanding of this process:

Example 1: People may not go through my personal belongings. Think about what core need isn't being met when someone encroaches on your territory. It could be a need for respect or privacy, or even personal space. It might even be all three.

HOW TO SET BOUNDARIES WITHOUT FEELING LIKE A D*CK

Example 2: People may not criticize me. What core need is at play here? It could be a need for respect or perhaps a deep-seated desire for acceptance.

Example 3: People may not make comments about my weight. In this case, the underlying core need might again be respect or acceptance.

Notice how many of these boundaries can be boiled down to the same core needs? It's interesting to see how interconnected they are.

Now, let's look at some examples from the second question in Step One:

Example 4: I have a right to ask for help around the house. What core need do you think this reflects? It could be a need for support, respect, or maybe both.

Example 5: I have a right to ask for more information before making a purchase. In this scenario, the core need could be time, space, privacy, or even respect.

I'm sure you're starting to get the hang of it, but let's do a couple more:

Example 6: To protect my time and energy, it's okay to turn off my ringer. The core need here could be time and/or personal space.

Example 7: To protect my time and energy, it's okay to change my mind. This is one of my favorites. The core needs here might include time, space, respect, and possibly even privacy.

As you work through this exercise, you'll probably notice that everything you wrote boils down to just a handful of core needs. Whenever you feel angry, taken advantage of, unheard, unseen, or misunderstood, ask yourself: which of my core needs are not being met?

Here are some common core needs you may identify for yourself:

- Respect
- Privacy
- Time

- Space
- Acceptance
- Support
- Safety
- Love
- Stability
- Freedom

You may have other needs that popped up for you, and that's perfectly okay—your needs are unique to you and are completely valid.

Keep this list handy as we'll come back to it in a few chapters.

CHAPTER TEN
Conditions versus Boundaries

"Walls keep everybody out. Boundaries teach people where the door is."
-Mark Groves

In the beginning, when we are first learning to express our needs to others, it's fairly common to unintentionally create *conditions*—or what I like to call Walls—instead of setting true boundaries. While these Walls might give us a sense of control and empowerment, they will ultimately isolate us and prevent us from creating the deeper and more authentic connections we crave.

In this chapter, I want to explore the difference between rigid, expectation-based *conditions* and flexible, negotiable *boundaries*. Understanding this distinction can help you ensure your needs are met without the risk of damaging your relationships.

The sad truth is, if people consistently seem to react negatively when you set boundaries, or if speaking up always seems to cause people to distance themselves from you, there's a good chance you have unintentionally been creating conditions without even knowing it.

CONDITIONS VERSUS BOUNDARIES

The Nature of Conditions

Think about all the times you've felt like you had to act or behave a certain way just to fit in, be loved, or be accepted. That's what conditions are.

Conditions are the rigid expectations we place on others. At their core, conditions are about attempting to control another person's behavior to meet our own expectations, and they are often enforced through punishment or negative consequences like shame, guilt, or the withdrawal of affection (e.g., giving the cold shoulder). Instead of allowing someone the freedom to be their authentic self, conditions demand conformity under the threat of subtle—or overt—punishment.

For example, let's say you have a friend, Alex, who is always late when you meet up. Frustrated, you start thinking, "If Alex really cared about me, he wouldn't be late all the time." You decide to tell Alex, "If you're late again, I'm going to leave and won't meet you anymore." While you might think this is setting an assertive boundary, what you have actually created is a condition—an ultimatum based on your expectation that people who care about you must always be punctual. This expectation most likely stems from past experiences where you felt disrespected or unimportant when people were late. By imposing this condition, you're subtly pressuring Alex to conform to your need for punctuality in order to feel valued and respected.

Or, let's say you have a partner who consistently leaves dishes in the sink, and clothes lying all around the floor. Feeling frustrated and at your wit's end, you might blurt out, "I'm sick and tired of you leaving your stuff everywhere. If you don't start helping out more around here, I'm done." While you might see this as setting a boundary, it's actually imposing a condition—an attempt to control your partner's behavior through the threat of actual, or perceived, rejection and abandonment.

This approach doesn't allow the other person the freedom to make their own decisions and learn from them. Instead, it imposes your expectations with severe consequences, fostering resentment and fear rather than understanding and growth. Although this might make your partner pick up after themselves, or your friend be more mindful of the time, the effects will likely be temporary and ultimately harmful to your relationship in the long run.

Conditions are typically rooted in our own fears, traumas, and projections and we impose them because, unconsciously, we are afraid of being hurt, rejected, or betrayed, or because previous experiences have taught us that certain behaviors are unacceptable.

For example, growing up, I was taught that if you truly cared about someone, you should always say "I love you" at the end of every phone call or interaction. So, when one of my boyfriends would simply say, "Okay, I'll see you later," I didn't see it as a normal goodbye. Instead, I interpreted it as a rejection, believing it meant he didn't care as much as I did. To ease my discomfort and feelings of rejection, I explained to him how much it meant to me to hear the words "I love you," hoping he would start saying it more consistently. While I thought I was expressing my needs, I was actually trying to control his behavior instead of having a genuine conversation about our individual comfort levels with showing affection. Rather than finding common ground, I set conditions that ultimately eroded trust and harmed our relationship.

Understandably, using conditions to get our needs met can seem effective in the short term, but can ultimately damage relationships by fostering resentment and creating an environment where power struggles and score-keeping thrive. Instead of promoting trust and mutual respect, conditions create an atmosphere where each person feels pressured to meet expectations—or else. Over time, this creates a cycle of chronic conflict and dissatisfaction, where everyone feels misunderstood and undervalued.

Types of Conditions

In your daily life, there's a good chance you will come across many different types of conditions that people impose on one another, often without even realizing it. These hidden expectations or demands for others to behave in a specific way to meet someone else's needs or criteria are surprisingly common and can be quite damaging.

CONDITIONS VERSUS BOUNDARIES

Here are some examples of conditions you might come across:

Conditional Affection: Conditional affection occurs when kindness or warmth is shown only if specific expectations are met. Think of the parent who only expresses pride in their child when they get straight A's or a spouse who is affectionate only when their partner cleans the kitchen or buys them flowers. This implies, "I love you as long as you make me happy." Over time, these conditions teach that love must be earned rather than freely given.

Conditional Approval: Conditional approval means showing support for someone's choices only if they align with your own beliefs. For example, a father who insists his daughter must go to law school feels disappointed and refuses to attend her graduation when she earns a degree in fine arts.

Such conditions attempt to stifle individuality and fosters a deep sense of inadequacy, often leading to feelings of unfulfillment and resentment.

Conditional Acceptance: Conditional acceptance happens when someone only welcomes or accepts you if you conform to their expectations. You can see a great example of this in the movie, *The Devil Wears Prada*, where Anne Hathaway plays Andy, an aspiring journalist who sacrifices her personal values, friendships, and even her relationship with her boyfriend to gain acceptance from her boss, Miranda Priestly, played by Meryl Streep.[16]

Conditions of acceptance use social pressure to coerce someone into suppressing their unique identity in order to fit in and earn approval. This can lead to intense internal conflict and a struggle to balance individuality with a desire to belong.

Conditional Attention: Conditional attention involves giving someone your focus only when they meet your needs or suit your purposes. For instance, the friend who only reaches out when they need to vent about their problems but is never available when you need support. Or the family member who constantly interrupts and diverts the conversation back to themselves whenever you try to share something important about your life.

These types of conditions create a dynamic where one person's needs consistently overshadow the other's, leading to feelings of invisibility and reinforcing the false belief that our worth depends on how well we meet someone else's expectations.

Conditional Love: This is one of the most damaging forms of conditions because love is such a fundamental human need. Conditional love happens when someone's love and affection are contingent upon meeting specific expectations or making the other person feel a certain way.

For example, a father might only show love to his child when the child achieves high grades or excels in sports. The child learns that love and approval are tied to their performance, leading to a constant fear of failure and a belief that they are only worthy of love when they succeed. This can result in deep-seated feelings of inadequacy and anxiety.

In romantic relationships, conditional love might manifest as one partner withholding affection unless the other conforms to certain behaviors or meets specific needs. For instance, a partner might express love and kindness only when their significant other dresses a certain way or agrees with their opinions. This can create a power imbalance, where the recipient of the conditional love feels manipulated and controlled, unable to freely express themselves or their true feelings.

Conditional love is often romanticized in movies, where love is shown to depend on fulfilling certain criteria. Take the musical *Grease*, for instance. Initially, Sandy doesn't feel fully accepted by Danny, who repeatedly blows her off and makes excuses for his behavior. It's only when Sandy transforms into the "sexy biker chick" that Danny is suddenly able to fully love her back.[17] This kind of love demands change and conformity rather than acceptance and authenticity.

The Trap of Conditions

Conditions affect more than just our close relationships; they also profoundly impact our connections with friends, parents, extended family members and colleagues.

CONDITIONS VERSUS BOUNDARIES

For example, in the workplace, a colleague might only support or collaborate with you when you agree with their ideas or take on tasks that benefit them. This dynamic can make you feel like you have to earn their cooperation by constantly putting their needs or opinions first. Similarly, in a friendship, one friend might only offer support when the other agrees with their opinions or follows their advice, making the relationship conditional on compliance. This dynamic can create an environment where connection and support are not freely given, but rather depend on meeting specific expectations.

Conditions create a subtle, constant pressure that can lead to fragile relationships, where everyone feels they must continually meet each other's expectations to be loved and accepted. This dynamic can cause significant emotional stress, anxiety, and a deep sense of inadequacy as relationships become transactional exchanges rather than the nurturing, supportive bonds they are meant to be.

To make matters worse, conditions often require us to use subtle tactics to influence someone else's behavior in order to meet our own expectations.

In other words, manipulation.

For example, saying, "If you really cared about me, you would do what I ask," puts pressure on someone to act against their instincts just to prove their love. This type of emotional manipulation uses guilt or the fear of losing affection to force compliance, which ultimately undermines genuine connection and respect; it creates an unbalanced power dynamic, where one person's needs are consistently prioritized over the other's autonomy.

Here's the tricky part: a lot of this happens without us even realizing it. Most of us don't intend to set conditions or manipulate others. In fact, many of us think we're so accommodating and *'Nice'* that we're the ones being manipulated! But the sad truth is that when we don't know a healthier way to identify and communicate our needs, conditions and manipulation become the inevitable defaults. While this may temporarily make us feel empowered and in control, it will lead to a lot of miscommunication and drama.

If you notice that the more you speak your truth, the more your relationships seem to suffer or drift away, it might mean you've unintentionally created conditions instead of boundaries.

So, how do we move beyond the constraints of conditional relationships and build real connections that are grounded in trust and mutual respect?

It all starts, or course, with boundaries.

Healthy boundaries are what allow you to create a compassionate space where you can teach others how to treat you—while still respecting their autonomy. When we have the courage to set clear, healthy boundaries, we communicate our needs and limits in a way that allows everyone to be their true selves, free from fear of punishment or manipulation.

Your Quick Reference Guide

Let's do a quick recap of the difference between *conditions* and *boundaries* so you can find this information when you need it.

Conditions:

Rigid and Imposed: Conditions are inflexible rules we set for others in an effort to demand compliance.

Enforced Through Punishment: They attempt to control someone's behavior by using shame, guilt, or by withdrawing affection.

Control and Manipulation: The goal is to make others conform to specific expectations.

Creates a Toxic Environment: Conditions foster resentment, create power struggles, and breed emotional co-dependency.

Example: "If you cared about me, you'd do what I want." or "If you don't give me what I want, I am going to leave."

Boundaries:

Flexible and Personal: Boundaries are adaptable limits you set for yourself.

Enforced Through Feedback: They use honest communication to maintain respect and understanding.

Fosters Autonomy and Respect: They encourage authentic connections without manipulation.

Creates a Healthy Environment: They promote safety, intimacy, and mutual respect.

Example: "I would love some time alone to myself to recharge," or "I would love to be spoken to more respectfully."

When Guilt Comes a Calling

As we wrap up this chapter, you might be starting to recognize areas in your life where you may have unintentionally set up Walls or conditions instead of healthy boundaries. If guilt is beginning to bubble up, know that it's okay. This simply means you are learning new things about yourself and becoming more self-aware.

The fact that you're here, reading this book, means you're already on the path to living a more authentic and compassionate life—and that's a pretty big deal. So if you're noticing things that could use some work, celebrate! Awareness is the first step to change, and recognizing these patterns is a significant milestone.

As we continue on this journey, be kind to yourself. Remember, this is not about perfection; it's about embracing your wonderfully messy, authentic human self.

Personal growth is a continuous process, and every small step you take towards understanding and implementing healthy boundaries is a victory.

CHAPTER TEN EXERCISE
Exploring Your Expectations

Expectations play a significant role in forming the conditions in our relationships. When we set expectations about how others should behave, meet our needs, or respond to us, they can unintentionally turn into rigid conditions that can destroy connection. Part of learning to set healthy boundaries involves recognizing where we might be unintentionally creating conditions in our relationships.

This exercise is not about judgment but rather about helping you explore different areas of your life to ensure conditions haven't accidentally crept in. By reflecting on and understanding your expectations, you can begin to identify where you can shift towards healthier, more flexible boundaries.

Take your time with this exercise and remember: it's an exploration, not an excavation. Conditions can be hard to spot, so be patient and thorough in your self-reflection.

Begin by finding a quiet, comfortable spot where you won't be interrupted. Grab a pen and your notebook or journal and take a moment to get settled.

Step One: List Your Relationships

Think about the various areas of your life where you have different types of relationships and make a list.

Include categories like Self, Kids, Partner, Friends, Coworkers, Parents, In-laws, Boss, Cousins, and anyone else who is significant in your life.

Step Two: Reflect on Expectations

For each person or relationship on your list, write down the expectations you have of them. Be honest—there's no judgment here. Use the following questions to help you explore your expectations more deeply:

CONDITIONS VERSUS BOUNDARIES

1. What do I expect from myself in terms of my behavior, appearance, achievements, and self-care?
2. What do I expect from my kids regarding their behavior, achievements, and how they treat me?
3. What do I expect from my partner in terms of support, affection, and shared responsibilities?
4. What do I expect from my friends in terms of loyalty, availability, and communication?
5. What do I expect from my coworkers regarding collaboration, respect, and work ethic?
6. What do I expect from my parents in terms of support, understanding, and involvement in my life?
7. What do I expect from other family members regarding their role in family dynamics and their support?
8. What do I expect from my community in terms of support, belonging, and shared values?

Step Three: Evaluate the Impact

Reflect on how these expectations may be influencing your relationships and your own health and well-being. Notice if they create pressure and tension or a sense of satisfaction and fulfillment. Look for any patterns or similarities across different areas of your life.

Some Examples To Get You Started

Need some ideas? Here are a few examples to get you started. Use these as a jumping-off point for your own exploration.

Personal Expectations

- Expecting yourself to always be perfect in every task you undertake.
- Expecting to achieve success and recognition in your career without any setbacks.

- Expecting to maintain a strict exercise regimen and diet without any lapses.
- Expecting to always remain calm and composed, even in stressful situations.

Expectations from Kids

- Expecting your children to get straight A's in school.
- Expecting them to always behave politely and never throw tantrums.
- Expecting them to participate in extracurricular activities and excel.
- Expecting them to show respect and obedience without questioning your decisions.

Partner Expectations

- Expecting your partner to always know what you need without having to ask.
- Expecting them to remember every important date and event.
- Expecting them to always be supportive and never criticize you.
- Expecting them to handle all household chores equally without needing reminders.

Friends' Expectations

- Expecting friends to drop everything and be available whenever you need them.
- Expecting them to always agree with your opinions and decisions.
- Expecting your friends to be supportive and understanding without you having to explain yourself.

CONDITIONS VERSUS BOUNDARIES

- Expecting them to initiate plans and keep in constant touch by checking in frequently, sending messages, or making the first move to maintain the connection.

Coworkers' Expectations

- Expecting coworkers to understand and support your ideas without any objections.
- Expecting them to meet deadlines and deliver work with the same dedication as you.
- Expecting them to maintain a professional demeanor and never engage in gossip.
- Expecting them to provide assistance whenever you need help without being asked.

Parents' Expectations

- Expecting parents to always agree with your life choices and decisions.
- Expecting them to provide emotional and financial support whenever you need it.
- Expecting them to be involved in your life without overstepping boundaries.
- Expecting them to respect your independence while being there for guidance.

Family Expectations

- Expecting other family members to mediate and resolve conflicts without taking sides.
- Expecting them to attend all family gatherings and events without fail.
- Expecting them to offer help and support during tough times without you having to ask.
- Expecting them to respect and honor family traditions and values.

Final Thoughts

Remember, boundaries have nothing to do with trying to control or change other people; they are about understanding and expressing your own needs in a way that feels good for everyone involved.

When we have too many expectations, we restrict people's ability to be themselves, creating relationships governed by conditions. By taking time to reflect on and understand your expectations, you can begin to transform them into healthy, sustainable boundaries that nourish both you and your relationships.

CONDITIONS VERSUS BOUNDARIES

CHAPTER ELEVEN
Stop Telling People How You Feel

"Your emotions are the most powerful guides you have. Trust them, for they reveal the path to your own heart."- Unknown

Now that we've explored your expectations to help you avoid inadvertently introducing conditions into your relationships, it's time to take the next step in our boundary-setting adventure: understanding your feelings.

Emotions play a significant role in setting healthy boundaries, yet many of us struggle to interpret them effectively. In this chapter I want to dive into the nature of your emotions, how they influence your boundaries, and how you can begin to harness them as valuable tools for personal growth and authentic connection.

By understanding the messages your emotions carry, you can learn to set boundaries that respect your needs and foster deeper, more genuine relationships.

What's The Deal With Emotions

If there's one thing we humans often struggle with, it's our emotions. No matter who you are or what you do, chances are you spend a good part of your day trying to push your feelings aside. But have you ever stopped to wonder what their purpose is? I mean, beyond making our relationships messy and keeping companies like Häagen-Dazs and Hallmark in business, why do we even have emotions in the first place? Think about it: we are evolutionary beings, and any traits or habits that don't support our species' survival tend to get bred out of our gene pool. Yet, somehow, emotions have remained.

Why do you suppose that is?

Believe it or not, your emotions are part of an intricate and complex communication system and they are at the heart of healthy boundaries. While, yes, they can be challenging and sometimes feel overwhelming, it turns out they are also key to successfully navigating our world.

From a biological perspective, your emotions are part of a sophisticated bio-feedback system designed to bridge the gap between your instinctual, unconscious awareness and your rational, conscious mind. This system translates your internal experiences and environmental cues into physical sensations and feelings, allowing you to understand and respond to your needs and desires more effectively.

Remember from Chapter 3 that your unconscious mind is the part of your mind that exists outside your awareness. Unlike your conscious mind, which is associated with the newer, more rational aspects of the brain, your unconscious mind doesn't have access to language to communicate. Instead, it relies on energy signals and physical sensations within the body to convey important information, acting as a bridge between your inner experience and your conscious perception.

Your emotions are part of the intricate language your neurology uses to communicate with you and they can offer important clues about what's happening inside you as it relates your immediate environment. By learning to decode your emotions, you can gain important insights into your needs and desires, which, as you're learning, is a key part of sharing effective boundaries.

The Biochemistry of Your Emotions

If we were to look at your body through the lens of biology for a moment, we would see that the human body is an intricate biochemical and electrical organism. Information moves through our nervous system in the form of electrical signals known as *action potentials* which are brief electrical charges that travels through our nerve cells.

Imagine your nervous system like a vast network of wires that carry messages all throughout your body. These wires, made up of nerve cells called *neurons*, send electrical signals to your muscles, organs, and tissues. This is what allows your brain to communicate with different parts of your body, controlling everything from your movement to sensory perception.

Here's the interesting thing: the nerve cells in your body don't actually touch each other. Instead, there's a microscopic space called the *synaptic gap* between every neuron throughout your brain and nervous system. Now, if you've ever explored electrical circuits, you know that electricity can only flow within a closed circuit. So how do those electrical signals move through your nervous system with all these tiny gaps all over the place?

This is where your *neurotransmitters* come into play. While you might recognize them for their role in antidepressant medications, they do so much more than just stabilize mood, and are a vital part of the functioning of your brain and nervous system.

Neurotransmitters are the biochemical component of your neurology and their job is to transmit and encode information as it relates to your immediate experiences. They consist of a diverse group of chemicals, including amino acids, peptides, and other small molecules that act as chemical messengers to bridge the gap between nerve cells, allowing the electrical information to pass from one neuron to the next.

Since electrical signals can't jump directly across the synaptic gap, neurotransmitters act like little ferries carrying passengers across a river, ensuring that signals keep moving in your nervous system. This means your emotions are not just random feelings or sensations that are meant to be ignored or repressed; they are valuable bio-feedback messengers that bridge the gap in your neurology, providing real-time insights into your internal state and its relationship to your external reality. Every time you feel a surge of happiness, sadness, anger, or fear, it's your body sending you signals about how your environment is impacting you. That's pretty impressive, don't you think? While we often try to brush off our emotions as meaningless annoyances, they are actually crucial for the functioning of our nervous system and for understanding our own needs and desires.

The Different Neurotransmitters

Just as you experience a wide spectrum of emotions, your body relies on a variety of neurotransmitters to relay information throughout your nervous system, with each one playing a unique role in maintaining your mental, emotional, and physical well-being.

Here are the most well-known neurotransmitters and their functions:

Serotonin: Often referred to as the "feel good" neurotransmitter, serotonin is responsible for helping to regulate our mood, appetite, and sleep. It contributes to feelings of happiness and well-being.

Dopamine: This neurotransmitter is important for motivation and reward and plays a vital role in regulating movement, motivation, and pleasure.

Norepinephrine: Known for its role in the body's "fight or flight" response, norepinephrine increases alertness and arousal, helping us react to stress.

GABA (gamma-aminobutyric acid): GABA is the brain's main 'calm down' signal. It reduces the activity of neurons, helping to soothe and relax the nervous system.

Glutamate: Glutamate is the brain's most common 'go signal' and is essential for learning and memory.

Your Emotional Reality Matters

Let's go back to the original question: what's the point of your emotions?

Given what you now know, it's clear why your emotions are such an important and powerful part of your biology. While it might be tempting to dismiss them as unimportant or "hippy-dippy" nonsense, the truth is they play a vital role in how information flows throughout your nervous system. Emotions, driven by neurotransmitters, provide real-time feedback about your external environment and its personal significance to you. They help you interpret sensory data in relationship to your life experiences, giving them meaning and context.

The problem is that most of us have been taught to label our emotions as either good or bad, with the ones that feel pleasant considered good and the ones that feel unpleasant labeled as bad. But if emotions are simply how your neurology encodes experiences, adds meaning to your life, and transmits information throughout your nervous system, then—biologically speaking—all emotions must be good, right? I mean, sure, some emotions can feel like absolute garbage, so it's easy to feel justified in labeling them as bad. But like it or not, emotions are a defining part of the human experience. When we label them as either "good" or "bad," we reduce the rich tapestry of information they contain into an overly simplistic, binary judgment that negates their true purpose.

The fact is, your emotions aren't inherently good or bad—they are simply neutral data in a sophisticated biological communication system.

Some of them just happen to feel super gross.

I know, I know... being human can be a total bummer sometimes. But, like it or not, a healthy person is meant to feel and experience all their emotions—even the icky ones. When we try to consciously repress our emotions, we actually disrupt the way information moves through our nervous system.

No wonder it wreaks such havoc.

So how do we fix this? The secret is to learn how to interpret your emotions and begin to leverage their insights to guide you.

The Hidden Messages of Emotions

If emotions are simply part of how information travels in your nervous system, and if each one is designed to convey important messages, wouldn't it be nice to know how to decode them? Well, you're in luck! Here is your cheat sheet to help you start unraveling the mysteries of some of the key emotions that might be showing up in your life.

Sadness: Sadness signals that there has been some loss or change in your internal or external world. Whether it's something big like losing someone important to you or something small like the coffee shop running out of your favorite drink, sadness draws attention to that loss. Its job is to help you process the experience and find deeper meaning in it. When sadness shows up, we naturally slow down, step back, and become more introspective. The purpose of feeling sadness, therefore, is to help us know when to pause and give ourselves time and space for healing.

When we mistakenly label sadness as 'bad' and judge ourselves for not being able to 'just get over it,' we miss the opportunity to use it as a signal that our soul needs soothing. By pushing away our sadness, we deny life's natural ebbs and flows and limit our ability to access an essential human trait: resilience. If, instead, we can learn to embrace our sadness when it shows up, we can process it, heal, and cultivate our ability to bounce back and grow stronger from life's challenges.

Fear: Fear is a signal that something is threatening your safety—physically, mentally, emotionally, or spiritually. Remember that you exist within four interconnected layers of reality, and the feedback from your emotions alerts you to changes or threats in any of these layers.

When fear shows up, it's your neurology's way of saying, "Pay attention: something dangerous may be afoot."

Often, when we feel unsafe, we look around at our external environment and tell ourselves that everything is fine, attempting to dismiss our fear as silly or irrelevant. We forget that the other three layers of reality—mental, emotional and spiritual—also need to be safe for our neurology to operate optimally.

Guilt: Guilt is a signal that we have acted in a way that contradicts our values and what is important to us. For example, if I accidentally step on your foot, I may feel guilty because I see myself as a good person who doesn't want to hurt others. My guilt is my mind's way of acknowledging that hurting someone goes against my values, prompting me to reflect on my actions and make amends if necessary.

Unfortunately, we often place too much value on what other people think of us. When this happens, we start seeking acceptance from outside rather than from within, leading to guilt whenever we try to prioritize our own needs. This guilt can keep us stuck in the cycle of being 'Nice' and constantly seeking validation to feel okay. But here's the truth: guilt was never meant to trap us in this cycle.

Guilt is meant to serve as a guide to help us realign with our values and what truly matters to us. It's not supposed to be used as a tool for self-punishment or as a way of seeking approval from others. When we understand and address the real source of our guilt, we can harness it to strengthen and reinforce our own personal integrity.

Grief: Grief is one of the most transformative emotions we experience because it forces us to say goodbye to parts of ourselves and step into the unknown. Much like the *Phoenix*, a mythical bird said to live for centuries before burning to ashes and rising anew, grief calls on us to let go of *Who We Were* so that we can step into *Who We Are Meant To Be*.

I often think of grief as an honored guest no one wants to host. Imagine receiving a call that the King of England is coming to dine at your home. You'd be honored yet terrified, knowing this visit would turn your life upside down. Grief arrives with the same power. It shows up uninvited and disrupts our sense of normalcy, demanding our attention. It comes as a wise guide during times of great change, insisting that we release a key part of ourselves that no longer fits in our evolving life. Grief asks us to endure the fire, to allow ourselves to burn down to ashes, and to find the courage to rise again.

According to Fred Luskin, a prominent psychologist and director of the Stanford Forgiveness Project, grief and forgiveness exist on a continuum.[18] Luskin's extensive research on forgiveness suggests that the primary goal of healing from grief involves not just experiencing pain or loss but also embracing forgiveness, both for ourselves and others.

Anger: Ah, anger—the most misunderstood emotion of them all. While most of us have been taught that anger is wrong, it is actually designed to communicate when you are giving too much or not receiving enough. It lets you know when something is unfair and alerts you to injustices in your world.

And—are you ready for it—your anger lets you know where you need to set boundaries. That's right—anger is your body's own built-in "Hey, you need to set a boundary" alert system! And yet, it is the first emotion we are taught to turn off because it's not "*Nice.*"

Oops.

Historically, it makes sense that we would be told that anger is wrong and makes us bad people. Since anger is our warning alarm for when we are being taken advantage of, it's no wonder those in power would want us to believe it's not okay. When we suppress our anger, it makes us more pliable and easier to control.

Anger is your own internal alarm that lets you know when your needs are not being met or when someone is crossing your boundaries. It lets you know it's time to say something and stand up for yourself.

For example, if you find yourself feeling angry because a coworker constantly interrupts you, it's your unconscious mind's way of letting you know that your core need for respect is not being met. Your anger isn't inherently wrong, it's simply a message letting you know it's time to speak up!

Unfortunately, most of us are taught to suppress our anger. We are told it is inappropriate and wrong and that being 'good' means being '*Nice.*' We are taught to prioritize the avoidance of conflict over the expression of our needs. As a result, we end up ignoring or bottling up our anger, which can eventually manifest as chronic stress, unexpected outbursts, and even physical illness.

In the widely popular book *Why Zebras Don't Get Ulcers*, author Robert M. Sapolsky talks about how suppressing anger can harm our physical health.[19] He explains that when we bottle up our anger, it triggers the body's stress response, releasing hormones like cortisol and adrenaline. These stress hormones can mess with our digestion, leading to chronic issues like indigestion, acid reflux, and changes in bowel habits. Sapolsky highlights how learning to express our emotions effectively is a key factor in our ability to stay healthy.

Putting It All Together

Let's look at how this all fits together:

If boundaries define your sense of *Who You Are* and your place in the world, and if anger is the emotion your neurology uses to signal boundary issues, that means anger is directly tied to your identity and your space in the world.

That's pretty important, don't you think?

When we are taught to suppress our anger, it might make us more pleasant to be around, but it comes at the expense of our own emotional reality. By swallowing our anger to be '*Nice*,' we trap ourselves in a world where we're not truly allowed to exist.

Yikes, right?

The good news is that by leaning into our anger, we can create space for the emotional aspects of *Who We Are* to exist.

Now, obviously, we don't want to vent our anger on those around us or walk around being constantly grumpy or rude. So, how do we honor our anger as the powerful self-alarm it is without wrecking our relationships?

This is where boundaries are invaluable.

With healthy boundaries, we don't have to walk around seething mad or hiding *Who We Are* to be '*Nice.*'

STOP TELLING PEOPLE HOW YOU FEEL

With healthy boundaries, we take responsibility for our emotions—without making them someone else's problem.

And it all starts with our anger.

CHAPTER ELEVEN EXERCISE
It's Time to R.A.G.E.
Release Anger Gain Empowerment

Let's face it: being a human can be downright infuriating some days. From traffic jams and long lines at the bank to the rising cost of living, there's plenty to get upset about. Add to that the challenge of sharing our world with people who were taught to be "*Nice,*" and you've got a recipe for a nuclear level of anger simmering inside most of us.

When frustration, annoyance, and irritation come knocking, you might think your job is to push it down and pretend you're "Fine" while secretly seething or complaining behind closed doors—but think again. Instead of bottling up those feelings, your new boundary-filled world involves acknowledging your emotional layer of reality and giving it space to exist.

And it all starts with anger.

This activity is what I call the *R.A.G.E. Dynamic Meditation.* R.A.G.E. stands for Release Anger, Gain Empowerment and it is a powerful way to channel your emotions and let go of stress and tension. Practicing this exercise regularly can help prevent emotional buildup and boost your emotional resilience, making it easier to handle life's ups and downs.

What's great about the R.A.G.E. process is how easy and quick it is. You can do it anytime, anywhere, and it only takes five minutes to complete. This means you can easily fit it into your routine without needing a significant time commitment. Whether you're at home, at work, or even in your car pulled over at a rest stop, this dynamic meditation will help to release pent-up emotions so you can regain your emotional balance.

For this activity, you'll need a pen, your journal or notebook, a timer (the one on your phone will work just fine), and your chosen instrument for the physical release (see options below). This is a two part process:

(1) Physical Release (2 minutes)

(2) Mental/Emotional Release (3 minutes)

For the physical component you can do anything that gets your body moving in some capacity. Some options include:

- Punch, squeeze, or pull at a pillow
- Scream into a pillow
- Strangle a towel or cloth
- Slap or whip a cloth against a hard surface
- Silent scream
- Fake cry
- Rip, crumple, or shred paper with your hands
- Hit or karate chop a pillow
- Squeeze a stress ball as hard as you safely can
- Dance to angry music
- Air punch
- Swing a foam bat
- Practice yogic breath of fire
- Throw soft objects at a wall
- Do an isometric towel pull
- Scribble violently on paper
- Bang on a drum
- Squeeze your hands
- Throw a toddler-style temper tantrum
- Stomp your feet
- Shake your fists
- Squeeze an empty bottle
- Blow bubbles vigorously into a cup of water
- Destroy a paper towel roll

When you are ready, find a quiet space where you won't be disturbed and take a few breaths to get settled.

HOW TO SET BOUNDARIES WITHOUT FEELING LIKE A D*CK

Step One: Release Physical Tension (2 minutes)

Set a timer for two minutes and then engage in your chosen physical activity (use the list above or feel free to come up with your own). Feel free to mix and match different options or combine them if you like, just be sure to keep your body moving for the full two minutes.

Step Two: Doing a Mental Brain Dump

After engaging your physical body, it's time for a mental brain dump. Set your timer for three minutes then grab a pen and your journal or notebook. Your job is to keep your pen moving on the paper for the entire three minutes letting your thoughts flow freely and writing down whatever comes to mind, no matter how silly or insignificant it may seem. Don't even worry about finishing your sentences! If in the middle of a thought your brain switches gears, follow it and just start writing the new thought.

Want to tell your coworker to go f#@k themselves but don't want to get fired? Write it in your journal! Have the urge to tell your kids to kiss your ass but don't want to traumatize them? Write it in your journal! Tired of your boss always making you work late or feeling sick of your in-laws' bullshit? Write it all out in your journal!

While your emotions might not always be socially acceptable, they are still 100% valid and real for you. These three minutes are your opportunity to get out anything that you've censored out of fear or societal obligation. You have full freedom to rant, rave, swear or whatever else comes up for you during this time.

Once your timer goes off, take a moment to reflect on the experience and notice any shifts or changes in your energy or emotions.

Remember, this practice isn't about fixing anything—it's about honoring your truth and giving your emotional reality space to exist. The goal isn't to make emotions go away, but to give them a voice. By doing this, you can avoid letting your emotions overwhelm you and risk damaging your health and relationships.

Some Helpful Tips for How to R.A.G.E.

I can appreciate that this exercise is likely outside of your comfort zone, and it's natural to feel a bit skeptical. However, I promise that giving voice to your truth on the emotional layer of reality can create powerful ripple effects in your life. To help you get the most out of this process, here are few tips:

(1) Avoid Making It a Workout:

It's important to note that the R.A.G.E. process is not meant to be a workout. The goal is not to exhaust yourself but to simply get your blood flowing a little to activate the physical layer of reality and help you tune into the emotions you would typically push down or ignore. Often, people tell me they can't do it due to physical restrictions which is why I have included many options that can be done sitting or even lying down in bed. The power of this is not in how much you move, only that you move with the intention of accessing your anger.

Another common excuse people use to avoid this process is claiming they don't need to release their emotions because they work out their anger and frustration at the gym or by running on the treadmill. While this may seem like a two-birds-with-one-stone scenario, it actually has the potential to create some unintentional problems: you might eventually run out of anger and lose your motivation to workout, or you may unconsciously begin to generate more anger in your life just stay motivated. Which means the happier you get, the less motivated you'll feel to take care of your health.

Oops.

If you do work out regularly, it's important not to use your workouts as your sole means of emotional release. Your workouts should serve a different purpose: they are for building strength, taking care of your body, and fostering a sense of accomplishment. Enjoy your workouts, but remember to process your emotions and do your R.A.G.E. release separately. This way, each activity can serve its intended purpose.

(2) Whatever Happens Is Perfect:

If you're used to being *'Nice,'* you might struggle to feel your anger initially, and that's totally okay. Whatever emotions arise—whether it's numbness, confusion, sadness, apathy, or guilt—are all valid and deserve a voice too. Even if it feels like you're just going through the motions and nothing is happening, trust that this process is working.

(3) Patience is Key:

If you've been burying your anger and emotions for what feels like eons, don't expect miracles overnight. It may take a few times before you begin to uncover the buried treasures and wisdom that awaits you, so be patient with yourself. Much like following a recipe gets easier and the cookies taste better each time you bake them, consistently working through this process will lead to more emotional breakthroughs and greater self-awareness.

(4) Always Set a Timer:

Time moves differently on the emotional layer of reality, so be sure to use a timer to keep yourself on track during your R.A.G.E. practice.

(5) Mix It Up:

Feel free to experiment with different tools and techniques. Don't like punching a pillow? No worries! Try scribbling furiously on paper instead. Does the idea of screaming make you squirm? That's okay! Try smacking a towel against a hard surface. Want to scream to an old 80's song while twisting bubble wrap? That's perfect! Your only job is to play around with this and find what works best for you. There's no one-size-fits-all approach, so feel free to explore and figure out what works and what doesn't. Some days you may want something more intense, while other days you might prefer something a little more gentle. All options are valid so just listen to what you need in the moment and choose the approach that best suits your emotional state.

(6) Embrace Imperfection:

The only way to mess this up is by not doing it at all. Seriously—there is no wrong way to R.A.G.E., so trust that whatever unfolds is part of the journey for you.

(7) Stream of Consciousness Writing:

When I say "put your pen on the paper and keep it moving for a full three minutes," I'm referring to a style of writing known as Stream of Consciousness. This technique, introduced to me by one of my creative writing teachers, trains your overthinking mind to step aside, opening a direct conduit from your intuitive self to the page. Engaging in this practice regularly will reveal surprising little nuggets of awareness that you can use to help guide you in your day-to-day and build your intuition.

Be patient—this process takes time. Initially, your thoughts might interfere, and that's perfectly okay.

You may worry about what to write.

You may worry about doing it wrong.

You may worry about it not feeling right.

You may worry about feeling silly.

You may worry about what others think.

This is all okay. In fact, it's a necessary part of the process. When these thoughts pop up, simply write them down! That might mean literally writing:

"I don't know what to write I don't think I'm doing this right this is dumb this is dumb dumb I can't believe I'm actually doing this I never do anything anything never never um um um how much time is left I'm tired I don't know where my coffee lid went missing behind the fridge did it maybe I don't know that's weird I don't know where that came um um um um..."

Whatever random thoughts, fears, words, or memories pop up, just write them down. If you get stuck and find nothing is coming up, simply write "nothing is coming up" or "I don't know what to write" or even just the word "um" over and over until other thoughts begin to bubble up. Remember, this isn't about creating a literary masterpiece—it's about dumping out all the random nonsense rattling around in your brain. Even if all you do is spend three minutes writing the word "f#@k" over and over again, that counts.

(8) Finding Privacy for Your R.A.G.E.:

Finding a private space to do your R.A.G.E. release can feel challenging, especially in a busy household. You might worry about your family hearing you and reacting negatively.

Here's a simple solution: the bathroom.

Yes, the bathroom! It's a private space with a lock on the door that generally offers a few minutes of uninterrupted time. If you're concerned about being heard, choose a quieter physical release option, such as strangling a washcloth, and then lock yourself in the bathroom for five minutes with your journal. It's not the most elegant solution, but it works!

Another option is to introduce this to your family. Kids, in particular, love engaging in this process—especially when they find out they have free reign to use whatever swear words they want during the full five minutes. If they are too young to write, simply give them paper and crayons and let them draw whatever they want during the mental brain dump portion.

Honestly, one of the best gifts you can give your kids is the permission to be human and to acknowledge their anger in a healthy way. Kids may not do what they are told, but they will model what is demonstrated to them. Show them what it means to honor your emotions by engaging in the R.A.G.E. process meaningfully yourself and then watch your family dynamic begin to transform.

A family that R.A.G.E.s together stays together!

STOP TELLING PEOPLE HOW YOU FEEL

CHAPTER TWELVE

Mastering the Art of Internal Boundaries

"When we are no longer able to change a situation, we are challenged to change ourselves."- Viktor E. Frankl

Phew—we've covered a lot of ground in the last few chapters, haven't we? But when it comes to understanding and holding healthy boundaries in your life, there's really no such thing as too much information.

By now, you should be starting to notice just how important your emotions are, and why allowing yourself to acknowledge and feel them is a superpower that should be celebrated, not repressed. Once you can really wrap your head around these concepts, stepping up and sharing your boundaries becomes so much easier.

So, the big question is: Now what?

Now that you know your core needs, how to source your own energy, how to identify when you are projecting, and how to listen to your emotions, it's time to tackle the art of setting boundaries without feeling like a gigantic jerk. And guess what? We're starting with the all-important boundaries you set for yourself.

In this chapter, I want to explore how to create boundaries that help you navigate your own internal landscape. These boundaries may not be as dramatic as shouting a firm "No!" at someone else, but trust me, they are the unsung heroes of the boundary world. The boundaries you hold with yourself create the standards and guidelines for your life, enabling you to live with greater clarity, peace, and self-respect. They are your own personal playbook for honoring *Who You* Are and how you want to show up in the world.

Your Personal Playbook

Imagine for a moment that you're the coach of a football team. While I might not be an expert in football, I do know that a team's success hinges not just on individual talent, but on how well everyone understands and executes their roles. This is where the team playbook comes in.

A playbook outlines strategies, defines each player's responsibilities, and provides plans for different game scenarios; it ensures that every player knows their position and how they contribute to the overall team effort. Without a playbook, the team would be disorganized, players would be unsure of their roles, and the game would be chaos.

Now, think of your life as a football game and yourself as both the coach and the player. Your internal boundaries are like your own personal playbook. Just as a playbook provides structure and direction to a football team, your internal boundaries give structure and direction to your life; they define your values, needs, and limits, allowing you to be able to navigate whatever life throws at you.

For example, a playbook helps the quarterback know when to pass, run, or hand off the ball, depending on the defense they face. Similarly, your internal boundaries can help you decide when to say yes or no, when to push forward, or when to step back, depending on the challenges you encounter. These internal boundaries ensure that you stay aligned with your true self, making choices that reflect your values and protect *Who You Are*.

So, what goes into your life playbook? What standards and guidelines can you set to make sure *Who You Are* is how you show up in the world? The beauty of it is that you get to decide!

Your internal boundaries are a reflection of your own unique values, needs, and priorities which means they are one hundred percent in your realm of control and fully up to you.

Think about what's most important to you. What values do you hold dear? What are your non-negotiables? These elements form the foundation of your internal boundaries. For instance, consider how you manage your time and energy. Do you allow yourself enough rest and self-care? Do you set limits on how much of yourself you give to others?

Knowing the answers to these questions is an important part of honoring *Who You Are*.

Boundaries and Energy Flow

Boundaries, whether they are with yourself or with other people, are ultimately about managing the flow of interactions, influences, and energy in and around us. They help us control what we allow into our personal space and what we keep out. There are four key ways we can do this:

(1) Deciding what to keep out, (2) Deciding what to let in, (3) Choosing what to keep for ourselves, and (4) Choosing what to share with others.

Let's go through these one by one.

(1) What We Keep Out:

When most of us think about boundaries, this is often what first comes to mind: keeping other people's draining, negative, *oogedy-boogedy* bad vibes out of our mental, emotional, and energetic space. The Bubbling and Grounding exercise you learned earlier (also known as *Energetic Shielding*) is an excellent example of managing this type of energy exchange. It helps to keep unwanted energy, like other people's criticism or judgement, out of your space and helps keep your neurology feeling safe.

MASTERING THE ART OF INTERNAL BOUNDARIES

(2) What We Allow In:

While it's true that boundaries often focus on what we want to keep out (like unsolicited advice or criticism), a big part of healthy boundaries also involves what we want to allow in—things like compliments or help and support from others. Sometimes, our boundaries are so rigid that they become like fortress walls, keeping us safe but also not letting anyone close enough to get to know us or help us when we need it. We'll talk about this more in later chapters when we explore the art of being receptive.

(3) What We Keep for Ourselves:

These types of boundaries are all about deciding which parts of ourselves we want to keep private. At this point we're starting to turn inwards and explore some of the internal boundaries you hold with yourself.

Believe it or not, you are under no obligation to share or explain anything to anyone–ever! While many aspects of our world are beyond our control, choosing what we keep to ourselves about our internal world is something we have full, 100% control over. And that's pretty amazing. Privacy is a fundamental human right. In an age where we are trained to share every thought we have with our friends and followers on social media, it's even more important to recognize and safeguard our right to the security of our own thoughts, beliefs, and values. Many of us have been taught that being *authentic* means we have to share everything and keep nothing private. But that's unhealthy too. You can be authentic and true to yourself, while still exercising discernment. This is not about being secretive or hiding things; it's about taking care of your own well-being and keeping what's important to you safe.

(4) What We Share With Others:

These boundaries help establish the standards and guidelines for our lives by allowing us to determine which parts of ourselves we choose to share with others. Here, we come to the heart of creating and holding internal boundaries with yourself. Just as you discern which parts of your life to keep private, you are also allowed to set standards around what, when, and how you share with others. This is about being mindful of how your truth impacts other people.

For many of us, we think it is our duty to share our opinions, advice, and feedback with others, believing that by doing so, we are being helpful. While well-intentioned, it's important to recognize that not every situation requires our input. Sometimes, simply listening and holding space for others is the most supportive and compassionate thing we can do.

A few years ago, I worked with a client who was struggling with her teenage son. She had done everything she could to help him, from writing letters to get him into university to calling employers to secure him a job. She gave him money whenever he needed it and made sure he always had the things she struggled to have when she was younger. Her intentions were rooted in love and a desire to protect him from the hardships she had faced. Unfortunately, by always jumping in to help, she unintentionally robbed her son of the ability to develop problem-solving and critical-thinking skills. He never had the opportunity to navigate life's challenges on his own, which led to him becoming increasingly anxious and withdrawn. His self-confidence suffered because he had never been allowed to experience failure and learn from it—therefore he didn't know how to succeed.

Through our work together, my client began to see the value in stepping back and allowing her son to face difficulties on his own. While she always remained available to offer guidance when asked, she learned to refrain from automatically jumping in with help or answers. It wasn't easy for her to watch him struggle, but over time she noticed small changes. Her son started taking more initiative, gradually building his confidence and learning to navigate life's ups and downs independently. Best of all, their relationship grew stronger as he began to see his mom as a trusted source of guidance, rather than a constant nag.

Too often, in our efforts to be 'Nice,' we try to solve other people's problems, unintentionally robbing them of an important gift: self-determination. The truth is, everyone has the right to try and fail; to do things their own way—even if it's the hard way. Allowing others the space to navigate their own struggles gives them the chance to discover their own strength and develop true resilience.

When we jump in with unsolicited advice or solutions, we might think we're being helpful, but we're actually undermining the other person's ability to find their own path. By consistently stepping in, we unintentionally send the message, "I don't trust you to figure this out on your own." This can erode the trust in the relationship, ultimately doing more harm than good. While our eagerness to help may stem from a genuine desire to share, it can also be driven by our need to feel useful or validated. We may jump into problem-solving mode without considering whether the other person actually wants or needs our input.

Years ago, I volunteered at an animal shelter where I worked alongside a woman named Carolyn. Carolyn was an incredibly keen, eager and kind soul who always wanted to help out in any way she could. Her enthusiasm was undeniable, but she unfortunately had a terrible habit of sticking her nose in everyone else's business. She would try to anticipate what everyone needed, often getting more underfoot than actually being helpful.

While her kindness was genuine, her lack of boundaries often made her a bit of a nuisance to everyone else. Instead of focusing on her own tasks, she would hover around, offering 'helpful' advice and jumping in to assist without checking if it was needed. This made it difficult for others to focus on their own responsibilities, and her constant interruptions made her hard to be around. As a result, people started to avoid Carolyn. They would go out of their way not to hang out with her, finding her overbearing nature overwhelming.

In her effort to be *'Nice'* and helpful, she had accidentally pushed people away.

Oops.

While the instinct to help is noble, sometimes helping without being asked can feel overwhelming and invasive, especially if the other person learns best by solving problems themselves. Having strong internal boundaries means setting standards around what we share and when. Moreover, having a playbook for how we offer guidance and support to others helps to preserve our energy for those who truly want our help or have given us permission to offer it. It helps us avoid the frustration and resentment that can come from feeling our efforts or input are unappreciated or ignored.

By setting internal boundaries with yourself, you can create a healthier, more balanced dynamic where your support is both meaningful and welcome.

Establishing Your Internal Boundaries

If you're still wondering how to use internal boundaries to guide you, let me share some examples inspired by my own journey. These boundaries are from my own personal playbook and have profoundly shaped my life. I invite you to adopt them as your own if they resonate with you.

(1) Boundary of Selective Ignorance: If something isn't said directly to me, I can choose to ignore it.

This type of internal boundary is all about maintaining my own peace of mind and avoiding unnecessary drama.

A few years ago, a woman I knew through networking was upset about something I had done, but rather than speaking to me directly, she decided to tell everyone else who would listen. Eventually, the story made its way back to me, and it was suggested that I go speak with her to clear the air. My response? "No, thank you." If no one had passed along the gossip, I wouldn't have even known there was an issue. If this woman really wanted to resolve the problem, she could have come to me directly. Her choice to involve others showed she was more interested in stirring up drama than finding an actual solution. So, I decided to ignore it and move on.

By setting this boundary with ourselves, we can save our energy for real issues and for people who value direct and honest communication.

(2) Boundary of Healthy Detachment: I'm not responsible for soothing someone else's emotional discomfort.

This type of internal boundary is all about learning to hold compassionate space for others without feeling the need to rescue or comfort them. While supporting our friends and loved ones is an important part of relationships, it is not our responsibility to fix or soothe someone else's emotions.

Remember that our emotions are an important part of how our unconscious mind communicates with us. This means, in those moments when someone is breaking down and overwhelmed with emotion, they are often the most connected to their own internal guidance. Sometimes, the most powerful gift we can offer is simply remaining silent and bearing witness to someone's emotions. If we jump in to help just to soothe our own discomfort at witnessing their emotions, we may unintentionally prevent them from finding deeper meaning in their experience.

Setting boundaries around how we offer emotional support is not just about protecting our own mental health; it's also about honoring another person's journey. By allowing someone the space to feel and process their emotions, you're showing trust in their ability to handle their own lives and grow from their experiences. More importantly, it allows you to hold compassionate space for others without getting dragged into their pain.

(3) Boundary of Permission-Based Advice: I only offer input or advice to people who have either asked or given permission.

This type of internal boundary is about conserving our energy for those who truly want and welcome it. Jumping in with unsolicited advice or solutions might seem helpful, but it can unintentionally overwhelm or frustrate the very people we're trying to support. That's why it's important to respect others' right to figure things out by only offering input or advice when they've explicitly asked for it or given us permission to share our opinions, feedback, or guidance.

People have the right to say no, make mistakes, and do things their way—even if we think their way is idiotic or misguided. Respecting others' right to make their own choices is essential for maintaining healthy and respectful relationships. By simply asking, "Do you want my advice, or do you just need to vent?" or "Is it okay if I share my perspective?" we give the other person a choice and show that we respect their autonomy.

HOW TO SET BOUNDARIES WITHOUT FEELING LIKE A D*CK

Setting this internal boundary with ourselves isn't just about avoiding offering unsolicited advice—it's about saving our energy for those who truly want our support. By waiting for explicit requests for our input, we conserve our energy for times when it's genuinely needed. This helps us avoid the frustration and resentment that can happen when our efforts go unappreciated.

(4) Boundary of Non-Interference: It's not my job to fix everyone's problems.

Similar to the last internal boundary about waiting for permission before jumping in to help, this one is all about giving others the space to figure things out for themselves. This approach not only builds trust and respect but also takes the pressure off you to constantly feel like you have to provide solutions. It allows you to honor another person's journey and let them navigate their own challenges while you offer support only when it's truly needed and welcomed.

(5) Boundary of Me First, Always: My needs must always be considered first before considering the needs of others.

This internal boundary is about ensuring we embrace the philosophy of being Self-*ish* in the best possible way.

While there's nothing wrong with caring about others, doing so at the expense of our own well-being is a big no-no. By putting our needs first, we can show up as our best, most authentic selves and offer genuine support without sacrificing our own health and happiness.

(6) Boundary of Looking Out For: It is not my job to look after people who are capable of looking after themselves.

This internal boundary is something many of us struggle with.

Often, in our efforts to show affection and concern, we cross the line from looking *out for* someone to trying to look *after* them, even when they are fully capable of taking care of themselves.

When we look *after* someone, we take on full responsibility for their well-being, often at the expense of our own. We manage their needs, constantly giving without taking time to replenish our own energy. This approach can lead to burnout because it creates a dynamic where the other person becomes dependent on us, and we feel obligated to keep providing support, no matter how drained we feel.

Over time, this imbalance can lead to resentment, frustration, and emotional exhaustion.

On the other hand, when we look *out for* someone, we provide support and care while maintaining our own boundaries and well-being. We recognize that our role is to assist and guide, not to manage their entire experience. This approach fosters interdependence and mutual respect, as both parties are responsible for their own well-being while also supporting each other.

Of course, there are some circumstances when someone may genuinely need us to step in and care for them, such as young children, individuals with health conditions, or those with physical or cognitive limitations. However, in most cases where we jump in to look after people in our lives, it's not because they can't do it themselves—it's because we don't trust them to do it, or we want to feel more in control to ease our own discomfort. This tendency can lead to unnecessary stress and imbalances in our relationships.

(7) Boundary of No Explanation Required: I don't owe anyone an explanation for my choices.

This internal boundary is about understanding that you don't owe anyone an explanation for your choices—ever. Just as in a court of law where you can plead the Fifth to avoid self-incrimination, you have the right to maintain your privacy and control over your personal decisions. While you might choose to share if you want to, you are under no obligation to justify yourself to anyone.

This internal boundary not only protects your mental and emotional health but also reinforces your autonomy; it allows you to live your life authentically—free from external pressures—and serves as a powerful reminder that your decisions are your own. Honoring this boundary in your life is the key to maintaining personal integrity and self-respect.

(8) Boundary of Permission to Change: It's your prerogative to change your mind.

This internal boundary is all about respecting the idea that life is a process of growth and evolution, and that we are allowed to change course whenever we choose. Just because you agreed to something initially doesn't mean you have to keep pushing forward if it no longer makes sense for you.

People change, circumstances change, and it's okay to adjust your decisions to better fit your life.

General Guidelines for Boundaries

As we move forward on this boundary-setting journey, I want to share some general guidelines to help lay the groundwork for the deeper work ahead. These principles will provide a solid foundation and ensure you have the tools and mindset needed to create boundaries that truly reflect *Who You Are*.

Your Feelings Are Clues: Emotions like anger, rage, hurt, complaints, or feeling threatened, suffocated, or victimized can reveal areas in your life where healthier boundaries are needed. Anywhere you are feeling these emotions—pay attention. That's where you need some better boundaries.

Embrace The Discomfort: When you first start to share your boundaries, you may feel weird, awkward, or unsure—and that's totally okay! These emotions are just your unconscious mind's way of letting you know that you are stepping outside your comfort zone and doing something new—which is a good thing, even if it feels a little strange.

Prioritize Your Needs: You cannot simultaneously set boundaries with someone and take care of their feelings. This is the one that keeps a lot of us stuck because we want to control how others feel and what is happening inside their circle. When you set a boundary, the other person may feel hurt, angry, or disappointed—and that's totally okay.

Remember, speaking up will likely require the other person to adjust their boundaries and move outside their comfort zone too.

Protect Your Privacy: No one can demand to know your thoughts or private business. Share what feels right to you, not what others expect. This is a big one for many of us who feel the need to unload every thought and emotion onto others in order to feel close to them.

Remember: you can be authentic and still have discernment and discretion.

Honor Your Individuality: Nobody has the right to tell you what to think, feel, or do—you have a right to your thoughts, feelings, values, and beliefs. Anything within your circle is yours and yours alone. Other people not liking or agreeing with it does not make it any less yours or valid.

Be Authentically You: You have the right to be *Who You Are* and live your life on your terms—as long as you do so with compassion and respect for others. Let go of guilt for not meeting others' expectations. Just as you can't control the circles' of other people, they can't control yours.

Accept Your Imperfections: You have the right to your imperfections and shortcomings without guilt. You are allowed to be human and perfection is never the goal.

Accept Yourself: *Who You Are* is entirely acceptable, just as you are now with whatever sensations, thoughts, and feelings you are experiencing.

CHAPTER TWELVE ACTIVITY
Creating Your Internal Boundaries Playbook

It's time to create some standards to help you ensure that *Who You Are* is in alignment with how you are actually showing up in the world.

In this activity, you are going to create your very own *Internal Boundaries Life Playbook*. This playbook will serve as your personal guide to help you stay true to yourself and *Who You Are*.

Start by finding a quiet space where you can be alone with your thoughts for a few moments. Have your journal or a piece of paper handy so you can make some notes for yourself.

Take a few deep breaths, and allow yourself to become more present in the moment.

Step One: Ask yourself the following questions. For each one, notice where your mind instinctively goes after you ask it, and then jot down your thoughts in your journal.

1. Where in my life do I tend to overshare?
2. Where in my life do I tend to stay silent?
3. Where in my life do I feel taken advantage of?
4. Where in my life do I feel like I am giving and not receiving?
5. Where in my life do I feel like I am receiving and not giving?
6. Where in my life am I not allowing myself to be seen, heard, or known?
7. Where in my life do I tend to downplay or minimize my accomplishments or worth?
8. Where in my life do I feel overwhelmed or drained by others' expectations?
9. Where in my life do I ignore my own needs to please others?
10. Where in my life do I feel unsupported or undervalued by those around me?

Step Two: Go back and read over what you wrote for each question. These will be clues—little nuggets of wisdom that can offer insight into where your internal boundaries might need strengthening. Based on your reflections, use the following prompts to create specific guidelines or standards for each area of your life.

Personal Boundaries: How do you want to manage your time and energy with friends and family? What personal space do you need to feel comfortable?

Professional Boundaries: What work-life balance do you want to help maintain your well-being? How do you want to handle interactions with colleagues and supervisors?

Physical Boundaries: What do you need to feel physically safe and healthy? How do you want to manage your personal space and physical interactions with others?

Mental Boundaries: How do you want to manage your mental health? What mental space do you need to think clearly and make sound decisions?

Emotional Boundaries: How do you want to handle your emotions and protect your emotional well-being? What emotional space do you need to process your feelings?

Financial Boundaries: How do you want to manage your finances to ensure your financial stability and security? What are your spending limits and saving goals?

Spiritual Boundaries: What practices do you want to use to nourish your spiritual well-being? How do you want to protect your spiritual space and maintain your connection to your beliefs?

Educational Boundaries: How much time and effort do you want to dedicate to learning and growth? What are your priorities in your educational journey?

Sexual Boundaries: What are your comfort levels and limits in your sexual relationships? How do you want to communicate your needs and boundaries with partners?

HOW TO SET BOUNDARIES WITHOUT FEELING LIKE A D*CK

By setting clear standards and guidelines for how you want to show up in the world, you send a powerful message about valuing yourself and your needs.

As you start to incorporate these internal boundaries into your daily life, remember to be patient with yourself. Establishing and maintaining internal boundaries is a continuous journey that grows and changes as you do. Keep your playbook flexible, adjust it when necessary, and regularly check in with yourself to ensure it continues to align with your evolving self.

Remember, each step you take towards honoring your needs and setting healthier boundaries brings you that much closer to living a more authentic and fulfilling life. Celebrate your progress, stay committed to your well-being, and watch how these internal boundaries can begin to transform your life from the inside-out.

MASTERING THE ART OF INTERNAL BOUNDARIES

CHAPTER THIRTEEN
The Boundaries Blueprint

"Speak your truth, even if your voice shakes." -Unknown

If you're still here and reading this, it tells me that you are serious about your boundaries journey and that you are ready to learn how to use your voice to inspire yourself and others—which is exactly what healthy boundaries are designed to do.

This is the crux of our journey together, the reason you are here.

Hearing someone speak up without malice or defensiveness is beautiful; seeing someone honor their needs without engaging in power struggles is inspiring.

Believe it or not, there's an art and a science to speaking your truth, and simply dumping your thoughts onto others isn't authenticity—it's chaos. In this chapter, I am going to teach you how to speak up effectively and compassionately.

This brings us to the heart of creating and sharing your boundaries: The Boundaries Blueprint.

What Is The Boundaries Blueprint?

The Boundaries Blueprint is a magical linguistic formula that allows you to feel heard, seen, and understood—without explaining, making excuses, defending yourself, or oversharing your feelings. This formula is designed to help you communicate your needs and desires clearly and effectively, ensuring that your truth is heard and honored, all while avoiding unnecessary drama or conflict.

And the best part? It's a single sentence. That's right—all it takes is a single sentence to share a healthy and effective boundary. If you've struggled in the past to assert your needs or express yourself without conflict, this blueprint is your ticket to transforming awkward conversations into moments of genuine connections.

The Boundaries Blueprint is just three simple steps and, when followed, will create a single sentence you can share.

Let's go through it together.

(1) Choose Your Supportive Starter

The first step in the Boundaries Blueprint is to set a tone of respect and appreciation by validating the other person's perspective and their experience. This is where you get to show empathy and compassion without having to take the other person's side or accept their opinion. To begin, select one of the following validating phrases:

"I appreciate"

"I respect"

"I agree"

"I love (you)"

Choose the one that feels most genuine for you in the moment, and then follow it with a statement that acknowledges the other person's perspective.

Here are some examples:

"I appreciate that you're really angry right now."

"I respect that you don't want to talk about this."

"I agree that this is something we need to address together."

"I love how passionate you are about this topic."

"I appreciate you were looking forward to hanging out today."

"I respect that you need these reports ASAP."

Beginning your boundary in this way helps to lay the groundwork for a meaningful conversation and shows the other person that you genuinely care about what they have to say. By starting with one of these opening statements, you can validate the other person's feelings and perspective to help ensure they don't feel attacked or defensive when you share your boundary.

The key to this step is sincerity. Avoid lying or making something up to sound '*Nice.*'

For example, if you think the other person's perspective is completely off-base and bat-shit crazy, saying "I respect what you're saying" is a flat out lie and will come across as completely insincere and fake.

Instead, simply acknowledging, "I appreciate that we have very different opinions on this," is enough to let them know you're paying attention.

(2) Bridge The Gap With "And"

Once you have established a foundation of respect, agreement, and appreciation by validating the other person's experience, it's time to bridge the gap to your own perspective. Do this by simply saying the word "and."

That's it – just say the word "and."

(3) Create Your Desire Statement

Now we come to the heart and soul of your boundary: sharing what you want or desire. This is your moment to express your needs clearly and confidently.

Start with the phrase "I would love" and then simply fill in what it is that you want.

For example:

- I would love to be treated with more respect.
- I would love my opinions to be considered.
- I would love to know that you are happy.
- I would love more time to think about this.
- I would love to leave the kids at home and go see a movie together.
- I would love to take next Wednesday off.

Putting It All Together:

Once you have completed all three steps, simply combine them into your boundary statement:

"I appreciate that you're really angry right now and I would love to be treated with more respect."

"I respect that you don't want to talk about this and I would love my opinions to be considered."

"I agree that this is something we need to address together and I would love to know that you are happy."

"I love how passionate you are about this topic and I would love more time to think about this."

"I appreciate you were looking forward to hanging out today and I would love to leave the kids at home and go see a movie together."

"I respect that you need these reports ASAP and I would love to take next Wednesday off."

That's it – you've created a boundary!

Tips to Make This Work

The Boundaries Blueprint is simple, but that doesn't mean it is easy. Many of us have practiced overcomplicating and making a mess of our boundaries for so long that the urge to complicate this process can be strong.

HOW TO SET BOUNDARIES WITHOUT FEELING LIKE A D*CK

Stay with me and I promise, once you get a handle on how this works, it will be easy to fit into your life.

Let's go through some important tips to help make this even easier for you.

(1) Avoid Starting with "I Understand"

Often, when we want to validate someone, we instinctively start with the words, "I understand" because it feels like a natural way to make the other person feel comfortable and heard. Unfortunately, for someone who frequently feels misunderstood or struggles to feel truly seen, these words can have the opposite effect. Instead of providing the comfort we intend, saying "I understand" may lead the other person to think, "If you really understood, you'd agree with me." This unintentionally shifts the conversation away from validation and can leave them feeling dismissed or unheard. Rather than fostering a sense of safety and connection, we inadvertently invalidate their experience right from the start.

Oops.

This well-intentioned but misguided approach can lead to frustration and disconnection, turning what could have been a constructive conversation into a defensive standoff or power struggle. This is why you'll notice that "I understand" is not one of the options in the first step of the Boundaries Blueprint. Instead, be sure to choose one of the four opening phrase options: *I appreciate, I respect, I agree,* or *I love (you).*

(2) Avoid The Word "But":

When you are transitioning from validating the other person's perspective to sharing your own needs, it's important to avoid using the word "but" and use the word "and" instead.

I know this might sound like a tiny, insignificant change and—trust me—it can make a big difference in how your message is received and understood.

In my private sessions and trainings, much of what I teach centers around the importance of linguistics and its role in shaping our perception. Remember that when those 11 million bits of information hits your neurology, it is your conscious mind's job is to gather as many details as possible and then weave them into a narrative that shapes your experience.

Just as the words we use inside our head are important and form the story we tell ourselves, the words we choose to use with others are equally significant. Small changes in our language can create profound ripple effects and, when creating and setting boundaries, it's incredibly helpful to have language on our side.

Linguistically, the word "but" negates everything said before it. Since our brains are wired to detect threats in our environment, when someone hears "but," they naturally tend to disregard what was just said and focus on what comes next instead. This means they will completely overlook the wonderful acknowledgement you just shared and instead feel like you're dismissing their perspective. Even if you're being totally sincere, using "but" can undo the validation you just offered in the first part of your boundary. Worse, saying "but" can come across as aggressive or confrontational—especially in highly emotionally charged situations. It can make the other person feel like you're challenging or diminishing their point of view, which shifts the tone of the conversation from openness to mistrust.

All because of one little word.

Suppose I say, "I want to go to the mall, *but* it's raining." With this statement, I'm implying that my desire to go to the mall is somehow directly connected to the weather. Now notice what happens when I change it to, "I want to go to the mall, *and* it's raining." By replacing "but" with "and," it now sounds like I am presenting two separate facts that can coexist without canceling each other out. With the word "and," the rain simply becomes a factor to consider rather than a dealbreaker—which is what is implied by the word "but."

Consider what happens if I say, "I appreciate your perspective, *but* I disagree." Here, using "but" can come across as though you're just paying lip service and don't really value the other person's point of view at all. By saying, "I appreciate your perspective, *and* I disagree," you can acknowledge and honor both perspectives at the same time. While this might seem like a small and trivial matter of semantics, I promise you that replacing the word "but" with "and" has a powerful impact on how your words and boundaries are interpreted—and received—by the other person.

Using "and" creates a space where both your opinions and the other persons can coexist; it linguistically shifts the conversation from one where only one perspective can be valid, to one where both viewpoints can exist together, without competition. Best of all, it opens up a shared space where your circle can overlap with another person's circle, creating the Vesica Piscis—a shared space—which is exactly what a healthy boundary is designed to do.

(3) Avoid Making Your Boundary a Command:

When expressing what you would love in the third step of the Boundaries Blueprint, it's important to ensure you avoid making it a command or a to-do list for the other person. You can do this by keeping the focus entirely on yourself and avoiding the direct use of the word "you."

For example, instead of saying, "I would love *you* to take out the garbage," which can come across as a command or an attempt to control the other person's behavior, you can keep the focus on what you want by saying, "I would love for the garbage to be taken outside." This rephrasing keeps it a neutral expression of your desire rather than a command or task for the other person.

This, quite possibly, is the most important part of this entire process.

Keeping the focus neutral and centered on what you want—without making it a command or demand—ensures the other person has nothing to get upset or defensive about. After all, you're not asking them to do anything or change; you are simply stating what you want. They still have a choice and are free to ignore you, but by speaking up, you at least give them the opportunity to understand your needs and respond if they choose. This simple linguistic shift can help to prevent misunderstandings and keeps the focus on your needs without provoking a defensive reaction.

Back when I was still working in animal hospitals, I had a colleague who had very different ideas on how things should be done, and our discussions would often turn into heated disagreements. One day, during yet another argument, instead of saying, "I need you to stop interrupting me," I instead said, "I would love to finish sharing my thoughts before we discuss them." I was completely shocked when this worked! Not only did it defuse the situation, it also felt so much better to share my needs in this way. I didn't feel like I was trying to control her behavior—because I wasn't. I was just stating what I wanted, and it was honestly a game-changer. This simple shift made such a huge difference by turning our arguments into more respectful conversations. Sure, we still disagreed (a lot!), but our disagreements stopped escalating into all-out wars.

By omitting "you" when expressing your needs, it can prevent your boundaries from sounding like commands or demands—which can trigger defensiveness or resistance in the other person. Instead, this method keeps the focus on what you need and helps to minimize unnecessary drama or conflict.

(4) Know Your Desires:

When I talk about your desires, I'm referring to those things you genuinely want in any given moment or situation.

The word "desire" often gets a bad rap, as if it's something taboo or something we should feel guilty about. But at its core, a desire is simply about what truly matters to you. It's not about what you need, what makes logical sense, or what you think you should do—it's about what you honestly, deeply *want*. Desires can be big, like achieving a major career milestone, or small, like enjoying a quiet evening with a good book. Whether it's wanting to learn something new, connect more deeply with loved ones, or simply enjoy the little things in life, your desires are those gentle reminders of what truly makes you feel happy and fulfilled.

Connecting with and expressing your desires is about more than just knowing what you enjoy or don't enjoy. It's about discovering what's really important to you—what truly matters. Your desires reveal a window into your Core Essence, and finding ways to give voice to them can help you live a life that feels more genuine, more meaningful, and more true to *Who You Are*. This is why sharing your desires is the crux of the Boundaries Blueprint.

(5) Avoid Making Desires Conditional:

When sharing what you want, it's helpful to avoid using phrases like "I need," which can make your desires sound like demands or ultimatums. Saying "I need" can feel rigid and implies that you can't function without getting exactly what you've asked for. This can create pressure, both for you and for the people around you.

A better approach is to remember to use the phrase "I would love." This simple shift in language makes your desires feel more like an invitation, rather than a strict requirement; it lets others know what you want without making it sound like a non-negotiable demand. Using "I would love" opens up possibilities and creates a more relaxed, positive space for others to respond with understanding and support.

In the beginning, speaking your desires out loud like this is going to feel a bit awkward, and that's totally okay. The more you practice, the more natural it will become. And the more comfortable you get with expressing your desires, the more you can notice that what you truly want will begin to show up in your life.

This is manifestation 101.

(6) The Secret 4th Step of Silence:

I know I promised that the Boundaries Blueprint was only three steps, but there's actually a secret fourth step that ties everything together. This is the key that truly makes the Boundaries Blueprint work. After you've delivered your single-sentence boundary, you absolutely, positively, must be quiet.

That's right – you have to shut up.

This is, quite possibly, the hardest part of the entire process.

When sharing your boundary statement, your job is to express it clearly and compassionately, and then remain quiet to give the other person the time and space they need to process and respond at their own pace.

This is the cornerstone of respect.

It is vitally important to let the other person speak first—no matter how long it takes. If you rush to fill the silence, you risk overexplaining or oversharing, potentially undermining the boundary you just set. You could also overwhelm the other person or interrupt their chance to think and respond thoughtfully.

So, state your boundary and then be quiet and wait.

If this feels uncomfortable, that's okay. Resisting the urge to fill the silence can be challenging, especially if you're used to filling conversational gaps. My advice? Find a way to keep yourself occupied—like singing a song in your head or counting ceiling tiles. Personally, I love to recite the lyrics to the song "Yakko's World" from the 90's classic cartoon, *Animaniacs*.[20] While the other person is considering the boundary I just shared, I'm silently singing in my head, listing all the countries of the world (hey, I told you I'm a nerd).

I know this might sound silly, but this step is more important than you can possibly imagine.

The difference between a boundary that works and one that doesn't often comes down to the language you use and the space you leave for the other person to consider your request. By remaining silent, you show respect for the other person's need to process. This is how you turn your boundary into the starting point for a meaningful conversation—which is pretty much the entire point of all of this.

The Boundaries Blueprint in Action

When you're first getting started with this style of language and communication, I know it can seem weird and a bit clunky. So, let's go through some examples together to help you get the hang of it.

Let's say you have a coworker who is super friendly but constantly interrupting you with questions they should be able to figure out on their own. You have a long list of things to get done and are getting tired of the constant interruptions, but you don't want to come off as rude. Instead of saying, "I understand you have questions, but I have work to do and need you to stop bothering me," you could use the

HOW TO SET BOUNDARIES WITHOUT FEELING LIKE A D*CK

Boundaries Blueprint and say, "I appreciate you have questions, and I would love to finish my work without any more interruptions."

Can you see the difference?

In the first option, the other person is likely to feel attacked or become defensive. Even if you're being super polite when you say it, you're basically offering a hollow platitude and then giving them an order. In the second example, however, you honor their need for answers while also clearly communicating your own needs. The difference is subtle but profound.

Let's go through another example together.

Imagine you have a child who absolutely loves to draw, color, and paint. One day, you walk into their room to find them drawing and painting all over their bedroom floor. After the initial emotional reaction, you need to go back and set a boundary. In the old paradigm, you might say, "Why would you do that? How many times have I told you to keep your markers and paint off the carpet." While this certainly gets the point across, it's not very compelling, and it essentially tells the child what to do (and let's face it, telling kids what to do rarely works and often makes them want to do the very thing we want them to stop doing).

If, instead, you use the Boundaries Blueprint, you can more effectively get your point across by saying, "I love how creative and expressive you are and I would love for all painting and drawing to stay at the table." Notice how this approach is clearer in setting your expectations while still validating the child's experience. It tells them what you want without negating their experience or making them feel responsible for your frustration.

Let's do one more.

Think about a time when someone was yelling at you or otherwise being loud, noisy, and obnoxious. Usually, in such situations, we might set a boundary by saying, "I understand you're upset, but you can't talk to me that way." While this lets the other person know their behavior is unacceptable, it doesn't clearly express what you do want—only what you don't want them to do. This can backfire because when we're already in a volatile situation, many people will dig in their heels and make things worse just to prove they don't have to do what they're being told.

If you, instead, use the Boundaries Blueprint, you could say, "I appreciate that you're upset, and I would love to be spoken to with more respect." This approach not only validates their emotions but also provides clear directions on what you want. While we cannot control what other people say or do, we can at least give them the choice by clearly stating our desires.

Remember that the goal of boundaries is to spark a conversation that allows both you—and the other person—to get your needs met. If we just tell people to leave us alone or what we don't want, we miss the opportunity to connect and problem-solve together, which is the glue that makes healthy relationships work.

This is the heart of authenticity.

This is how we allow *Who We Are* to become a bridge to deeper connections.

Go Beyond Boundaries

While the Boundaries Blueprint formula is great for sharing your boundaries, feel free to use it in other situations as well. In fact, it's an excellent way to get comfortable with the language and practice the formula in your daily life. This way, when you need it for a boundary, it will be second nature.

For example, when ordering your morning coffee, you could say, "I appreciate you taking my order, and I would love a large non-fat latte." Or, when deciding what to do after dinner, you might express, "I love how beautiful it is outside, and I would love to go for a walk around the neighborhood."

Feel free to play with the Boundaries Blueprint and practice weaving it into your everyday life. The more you use the formula, the easier it becomes to share what you want with the world.

If you're still in need of some inspiration, here are some more examples of 'I would love' desire statements that might come in handy:

HOW TO SET BOUNDARIES WITHOUT FEELING LIKE A D*CK

- "I would love to be spoken to more gently."
- "I would love some reassurance that we are okay."
- "I would love to spend the holidays quietly at home."
- "I would love to have a conversation about my salary."
- "I would love all the toys cleaned up before dinner."
- "I would love for assignments to be submitted on time."
- "I would love to hold hands more."
- "I would love someone else to do the dishes when I cook."
- "I would love to take a walk together after dinner."
- "I would love to have a dedicated time for our weekly meetings."
- "I would love to receive feedback on my performance."
- "I would love to be listened to without interrupting."
- "I would love to plan a weekend getaway together."
- "I would love to see everyone arrive on time for family events."
- "I would love to have a clear plan for our project."
- "I would love to have a no-phone policy during meals."
- "I would love to feel more supported in my decisions."
- "I would love to spend more quality time together."
- "I would love to have my efforts acknowledged more often."
- "I would love to discuss our future plans together."
- "I would love to have my feedback considered and shared with the team."

Remember—keep your "I would love" statements neutral and without the word "you." This keeps the focus on _your_ desires and avoids turning them into commands or to-do lists.

What Happens Next?

Great! You've spoken up and shared your boundary statement using the Boundaries Blueprint—woo hoo! Now what?

After sharing your boundary, be prepared for a few different reactions from the other person.

(1) Acceptance and Understanding:

The other person may immediately understand and respect your boundary, appreciate your honesty and agree to honor your request.

This positive response indicates a relationship built on a strong foundation of mutual respect and understanding and is a sign that, in this instance, your values align perfectly.

If this happens, celebrate—you're done!

(2) Confusion or Rejection:

The other person might be taken aback or confused by your boundary, especially if it's the first time you've ever spoken up or asserted it. They may need time to process what you've shared or may ask for some clarity.

Alternatively, they might reject your boundary outright, react defensively, and choose to end the conversation. In this case, it's important to respect their decision to leave, recognizing that their rejection does not diminish the validity of your boundary.

Remember, the goal of speaking up is to give your desires a voice and to hear yourself express them—regardless of the other person's response.

(3) Resistance or Pushback:

Sometimes when you share your boundaries, you might encounter resistance or pushback. This can happen when what you want and value clashes with what the other person wants and values, or when your boundary pushes them out of their comfort zone. When this happens, they might try to dismiss your boundary with what I like to call a "Yeah, but." This is where you share your boundary, and they respond with "Yeah, but..." followed by all the reasons why you're wrong.

If this happens, rest assured that this reaction is a completely normal and natural way for someone to assert their viewpoint. It doesn't mean they're a bad person—it just means they weren't prepared for your request and are trying to make their side more clear. This is what makes sharing your boundaries a conversation rather than a one-way demand.

Even if it feels frustrating, it's actually a good thing.

Responding to Resistance

When you encounter a "Yeah, but" or any other form of resistance, it's natural to feel a bit deflated. But remember, this is your boundary, not theirs, which means they are under no obligation to accept or agree with it. Their resistance doesn't invalidate your desires—it simply highlights the importance of sharing your perspective. Whether or not the other person agrees or responds the way you hoped, the important thing is that you've spoken up and shared what you want.

So, what do you do when you encounter resistance to your boundary?

When faced with a "Yeah, but"—or any other defensive response—it's important to stay quiet and let the other person finish sharing their perspective. Even if their words make you want to scream or lash out—remain calm and silent until they are done speaking. Once they stop talking, calmly respond by saying, "Yes, and I would love..." and then repeat your desire statement. Alternatively, if it feels more appropriate, you can say, "I hear you, and I would love..." followed by your desire statement.

That's it. That's all there is to it.

When you consistently respond with phrases like, "Yes, and I would love..." or "I hear you, and I would love..." the conversation will naturally shift toward negotiation and collaboration—or it will come to a conclusion and end.

Here's a sample conversation:

Me: "I appreciate you are tired, and I would love to figure this out."

Them: "Yeah, but I have to wake up early tomorrow, and I don't want to deal with this now."

Me: "I hear you, and I would love to figure this out."

Them: "Well I don't – which you obviously don't even care about."

Me: "I hear you and I would love to figure this out."

Them: "I'm not doing this tonight but how about we figure it out first thing in the morning."

Me: "I am okay with that."

This consistent approach helps reinforce your boundary without getting sucked into an argument; it stops you from feeling the need to overexplain or justify what you want and instead simply reaffirms your desire. As you continue this strategy, eventually, the conversation will either come to an end or lead to negotiation, which we'll discuss more in the next chapter. For now, it's important to understand that using this formula allows you to respond without engaging in conflict.

It lets you respect the other person's viewpoint while also clearly stating your own needs and desires.

A Point of Clarification

I want to be clear, saying "Yes, and" when faced with resistance doesn't mean you agree with what the other person is saying, especially if they resort to name-calling or disrespectful behavior. Instead, saying "Yes, and" simply acknowledges their thoughts and feelings.

This is about validation, not agreement.

Keep in mind, it is not your job to make the other person more respectful. Your job is to ensure you are heard, even if they are choosing to be disrespectful or toxic. By using "Yes, and," you validate the other person's perspective, which can help de-escalate the situation while still standing firm on your boundaries.

HOW TO SET BOUNDARIES WITHOUT FEELING LIKE A D*CK

More Helpful Examples:

If you're still wrapping your head around this, here are some more helpful examples to illustrate how to use the Boundaries Blueprint in various scenarios and with the different people in your life:

With Your Partner:

"I appreciate you're really angry right now, and I would love to have this conversation more calmly."

"I love you and I would love to go away somewhere special together."

"I agree that we need to address this together, and I would love to consider other alternatives."

With a Family Member:

"I love how passionate you are about this topic, and I would love to be spoken to at a lower volume."

"I appreciate you were looking forward to hanging out today, and I would love to stay home and rest."

"I respect your opinion on this matter, and I would love the opportunity to make my own decisions."

With a Coworker:

"I respect that you need these reports ASAP, and I would love to discuss extending the deadline by a few days."

"I appreciate your feedback on my project, and I would love specific examples to improve my work."

"I agree that collaboration is important, and I would love to set some boundaries for our meetings to stay on track."

With Your Boss:

"I appreciate your dedication to the project, and I would love to have a better work-life balance."

"I respect your decision, and I would love to have a conversation about my role and responsibilities."

"I agree that this task is a priority, and I would love to discuss the resources needed to complete it efficiently."

With a Teacher:

"I appreciate your commitment to helping us learn, and I would love to have more clarity on the assignment guidelines."

"I respect your expertise, and I would love some additional support with this topic."

"I agree that attendance is important, and I would love to discuss the reasons for my recent absences."

With Your Child:

"I appreciate that you want to stay up late, and I would love for bedtime to be respected."

"I respect your feelings about homework, and I would love to help create a study schedule."

"I agree that playing is fun, and I would love for all the toys to be cleaned up afterward.

With a Teenager:

"I appreciate your desire for independence, and I would love to agree on some basic house rules."

"I respect that you want to spend time with your friends, and I would love to be kept in the loop on your plans."

"I agree that personal space is important, and I would love for all food to be kept out of bedrooms."

A Recap of The Boundaries Blueprint

Need a quick refresher? Here's the step-by-step guide to create your boundary statement.

(1) Start with "I appreciate/I respect/I agree/I love (you)"

(2) Connect the thought with "and"

(3) Share your desire by saying "I would love..."

(4) Stay quiet and listen.

If you encounter resistance, respond with "Yes, and I would love…" or "I hear you, and I would love…" until a deeper conversation emerges.

THE BOUNDARIES BLUEPRINT

CHAPTER THIRTEEN ACTIVITY
Mapping Out Your Boundaries

Now that you've learned the Boundaries Blueprint, it's time to put it into action by mapping out your boundaries on paper. Why? Because the more you can understand your wants and desires ahead of time, the easier it is to share authentically in the moment. Writing out your boundaries can help you clarify your thoughts and feelings, ensuring that you communicate them effectively when the time comes. Plus, having a written reference can boost your confidence and reinforce your commitment to honoring your own needs.

For this activity, all you need is a pen, your journal or notebook and a few quiet moments to yourself.

Step One: Identify Five Key Relationships

Choose five of the most important relationships in your life that you want to focus on for this exercise. These should be relationships where you've noticed a need for clearer boundaries or where you want to strengthen communication. Consider the areas where you feel the most tension or where misunderstandings frequently occur.

Some options could include: Mother, Father, Siblings, Children, Partner, Boss, Coworker, Employees, Friends, or even neighbors. By identifying these key relationships, you can tailor your boundary-setting efforts to the areas that will have the most impact on your overall well-being and relational health.

Step Two: Revisit Your Core Needs

Revisit the Core Needs you identified in Chapter 9 as these will serve as the foundation for your boundaries. Examples of Core Needs include personal space, time, emotional support, respect, and privacy. Being aware of your Core Needs makes it easier to create your "I would love" statements and you can use your Core Needs as a starting point to help you determine what you want or desire in each situation.

THE BOUNDARIES BLUEPRINT

Step Three: Map Out Your Boundaries

For each of the five relationships you selected, create a simple chart or list with three columns:

<u>Column One:</u> Write down the name of the person or their relationship to you (i.e., Mom, Dad, Sister, Brother, Friend, Co-Worker...etc.)

<u>Column Two:</u> Write down your Core Need (i.e., Time, Space, Support, Respect, etc.).

<u>Column Two:</u> For each person and core need, jot down 3-5 statements of what you desire by starting with "I would love."

Relationship	Core Need	Desire Statement
Best Friend	Time	I would love to set aside one weekend a month for our get-togethers. I would love to have our phone calls after 7:00pm when I'm more relaxed. I would love to have some time to myself on Sunday afternoons. I would love for our get togethers to happen at the time we agreed upon

HOW TO SET BOUNDARIES WITHOUT FEELING LIKE A D*CK

Relationship	Core Need	Desire Statement
Parents	Respect	I would love to be spoken to with more respect I would love for my decisions to be respected I would love to be given the benefit of the doubt I would love to feel supported in my life choices

Step Four: Write Down Your Boundaries:

Once you've mapped out your desire statements for each relationship, take some time to write them down clearly and concisely using the Boundaries Blueprint formula.

To do so, create the following chart in your journal or notebook and then fill in each column:

Who I will be sharing these Boundaries with	I appreciate/I respect I agree/I love	AND	I would love

THE BOUNDARIES BLUEPRINT

For example:

Who I will be sharing these Boundaries with	I appreciate/I respect I agree/I love	AND	I would love
Best Friend	I appreciate that we both have busy schedules	and	I would love to have our phone calls after 7:00pm when I'm more relaxed
Parent	I respect that you like to talk in the afternoon	and	I would love for my decisions to be respected

Here are some other examples to inspire you:

I appreciate that you were only a few minutes late, and I would love for our get togethers to happen at the time we agreed upon.

I agree that this is frustrating and I would love to be spoken to with more respect.

I appreciate you don't approve of my choices and I would love for my decisions to be respected.

I love you and I would love to be given the benefit of the doubt.

I appreciate that this is not something you would choose for yourself, and I would love to feel supported in my life choices.

HOW TO SET BOUNDARIES WITHOUT FEELING LIKE A D*CK

Step Five: Review and Reflect:

Once you have created your boundary statements using the Boundaries Blueprint, take some time to review your list for each relationship.

You might find that some boundaries work across multiple relationships, so feel free to mix and match.

Remember to check for any linguistic traps such as the word "but" or "I would love <u>you</u>" and ensure your boundary statements focus on your own needs and desires without placing demands or conditions on the other person.

As you review your boundaries, ask yourself the following questions:

- Do these boundaries reflect my core values and priorities?
- Do they clearly share what I want (as opposed to what I <u>don't</u> want)?
- Have I avoided any language that could be perceived as confrontational or conditional?

Taking the time to create and review your boundaries ensures they truly align with *Who You Are* and what you genuinely want in your relationships. It also sets the stage for more open and honest communication, allowing you to speak up while still maintaining your integrity and self-respect.

Step Six: Practice Makes Better

Finally, practice stating your boundaries out loud. This will help you become more comfortable and confident with the language, making it easier to express your boundaries when the time comes. You might even want to role-play with a trusted friend, family member or your coach or counsellor to get feedback and refine your approach.

By preparing in this way, you're not only reinforcing your own commitment to your boundaries, you're also ensuring that you're ready to communicate them effectively when you need to.

Troubleshooting Tips

Since this is a new skill, there's a good chance you'll stumble at bit at first, maybe tripping over your words or unintentionally adding in a "but" or two in the beginning.

I want to assure you—this is okay! If you find yourself struggling, here are some tips to help you get back on track.

(1) If You Say It Wrong, Just Say It Right:

Learning to set boundaries and communicate effectively is a skill that takes time and practice to fully develop. In the beginning, there's a good chance you will botch the formula the first few times you use it. And that's totally okay! If you catch yourself saying something incorrectly—just correct it. Even if you're in the middle of the statement and notice things going awry, stop and start again.

For example, it's perfectly okay to say, "I understand where you're coming from but... I mean, I appreciate where you're coming from and...." Trust me, the other person likely won't even notice. So if halfway through stating your boundary you need a do-over, just stop and start again. It's totally fine!

(2) There's No Failure, Only Feedback:

Be gentle with yourself as you practice this new way of communicating and know that each time you use this formula—even if it's not perfect—you're training your brain and attuning it to healthier communication patterns. And that's a big deal. At first, you will likely only realize the need for a boundary after the moment has passed. When that happens—celebrate! This new awareness is a big step. Each time you notice where a boundary is needed and make an effort to practice new ways to share it, you're reinforcing the habit of clear and effective boundary-setting.

So, if you don't catch every situation or get it perfect right away, that's totally fine. What matters most is that you're making an effort to communicate more authentically and respectfully. Just keep practicing, and soon it will become second nature.

(3) Growth Feels Uncomfortable:

Above all, be kind to yourself as you embark on this journey of setting boundaries and self-growth. Learning to set healthy and effective boundaries is a new skill, so it's perfectly normal to feel a bit uncomfortable or awkward at first. Remember that a healing wound doesn't always feel good—it often itches and feels strange as it mends. In the same way, using boundaries as a healing tool in your life might feel a little weird at first, but that's just part of the process.

Stick with it and then watch the magic happen.

THE BOUNDARIES BLUEPRINT

CHAPTER FOURTEEN

The Art of Compassionate Negotiation

"Negotiation and discussion are the greatest weapons we have for promoting peace and development." – Nelson Mandela

In the last chapter, you learned the Boundaries Blueprint—a magical formula that allows you to share your needs and desires in a way that encourages connection and collaboration. I also hinted that this process is designed to lead to deeper, more meaningful conversations, and that, by consistently validating the other person, you can create a space for genuine dialogue and collaboration.

In this chapter, I want to dive deeper into the transformative potential of the Boundaries Blueprint by exploring the art of compassionate negotiation.

This is about being able to recognize that when two people's perspectives overlap, it creates a shared space where neither person's viewpoint dominates. In this space, both individuals can come together and allow their desires to merge, creating something greater than what either could achieve alone.

It is in this shared space that true negotiation can happen.

Taking Your Boundaries Deeper

After you have shared your boundary sentence, and repeated the "Yes, and I would love..." statement two or three times, a deeper conversation will often begin to emerge. The other person may start asking questions or otherwise indicate a shift from defensiveness to curiosity and a willingness to understand your perspective.

For example, several years ago, a client came to me whose father was not very supportive of her life choices. After many years of fighting, with each trying to convince the other why they were right, my client decided to use a different approach. Using the Boundaries Blueprint formula, she shared the following boundary with her dad:

"I appreciate that you don't agree with my life choices, and I would love to feel supported by my father."

Predictably, her father initially got extremely upset and defensive—shouting, bringing up past issues, and even throwing out a few insults. My client stayed quiet, and when it was her turn to speak, she calmly repeated: "Yes, and I would love to feel supported by my father." Once again, her father ranted and raved, while my client patiently waited (she later told me she was reciting the lyrics to a song from the Broadway musical, *Wicked*[21] in her head). After repeating her "Yes and I would love" statement for the third time, her father finally broke down and yelled, "I just don't know how to support you!"

This was a revelation for them both.

Sharing in this way opened the space for a deep and profound conversation in which her father not only expressed his own insecurities but also apologized for not being as supportive as my client had needed over the years. By using these linguistic tools to share her boundary, she was able to create a meaningful connection that was validating for both of them and, together, they were able to come up with a plan that felt good for him and supportive for her.

According to my client, that one conversation completely transformed their entire relationship.

This is the power of boundaries. When you use the right language, they can become profound tools for building stronger and more fulfilling relationships.

Conflict as a Conduit To Connection

Often, when you share your boundary, it won't be met with immediate agreement or open arms. In fact, most of the time, your boundary is going to encroach on someone else's space, triggering a need for a deeper conversation.

For example, if you tell your roommate you need quiet time in the evenings to unwind, they might feel like their social time is being restricted. This reaction is normal and just means it's time to talk things through.

The reality is, someone disagreeing with or challenging your boundary isn't necessarily a sign of disrespect or dismissal, nor does it mean the relationship is doomed or that the other person doesn't care about you. It's simply a natural part of human interaction where your boundaries meet and intersect with another person's boundaries. Disagreements or challenges to your boundaries are simply signs that your needs and values are intersecting with someone else's. This intersection isn't inherently bad or negative; it's simply an opportunity to understand each other's perspectives and find common ground. When this overlap happens means that your circles are beginning to intersect, creating a shared space—the Vesica Piscis—where new possibilities can emerge. In this shared space, you have the ability to actually get to know someone and create a deeper bond.

For instance, let's say you set a boundary with a friend about needing personal space on weekends. If your friend challenges this boundary by asking you to hangout on a Saturday together, it doesn't mean they don't respect your needs. Instead, it means their need for connection is intersecting with your need for space. This is a moment to explore these overlapping needs and find a solution that honors both of you. These moments of overlap call on us to experience more of *Who We Are* and can be a powerful conduit for deeper and more meaningful relationships. If you run away at the first sign of invalidation, resistance or disagreement, you could unintentionally rob yourself—and the other person—of a valuable opportunity to create something truly beautiful together.

The key is to approach these moments with curiosity and to continue using effective communication skills to navigate the conversation. After all, you've worked hard to share your boundary! You don't want to accidentally undo it and get dragged into unnecessary drama. You also don't want to undermine your efforts by compromising on the desire you've courageously shared. So, what's the secret?

Stop relying on compromise as your sole means of resolving disagreements and instead embrace the art of *compassionate negotiation*.

This is conflict resolution 101.

Compromise Vs. Negotiation

When it comes to resolving conflicts and making sure everyone's needs are met, we often think of two main approaches: negotiation and compromise. While both aim to find common ground, they differ fundamentally in how they get there.

Compromise is often seen as the be-all-and-end-all, ultimate, go-to solution for conflict resolution. It's the one we are taught from a very young age and it is fully focused on everyone being 'Nice.' Compromise is essentially a conflict-avoidance strategy that involves each person giving up something they want in order to reach an agreement. Everyone involved is expected to offer a personal sacrifice for the purpose of appeasing the group as a whole.

In a compromise, both sides win a little and lose a little. Sure, it may stop the conflict, but it often leaves neither side fully happy because everyone has had to sacrifice at least part of their desires or needs just to keep the peace. This can result in feelings of bitterness and resentment—which isn't so great for relationships.

For example, let's say I want to paint the front door of our house red, while my husband wants to paint it black. In a compromise, we might agree that if I get to choose the color for the front door of the house, then he can choose the color for the garage door and I don't get any say in the matter. While this seems fair on the surface—we each get to choose a door's colour—it doesn't actually uncover the underlying reasons why each of us prefers our chosen colors. We learn nothing new about each other, and we both walk away with partial wins and losses, trying to match our levels of misery rather than achieving true mutual satisfaction. Understandably, this style of communication can easily lead to score-keeping, as every time we pass by the doors we don't like, we're reminded of not getting something we wanted.

Compassionate negotiation, on the other hand, focuses on creating new options that meet everyone's needs. It's not about splitting the difference, but about deeply understanding each other's motivations to find common ground and come up with new solutions.

How do we do this? All you have to do is ask better questions.

Asking Better Questions

In earlier chapters, we discussed how the conscious mind functions like a spotlight, shining on the actors on a stage, while the unconscious mind operates more like the backstage crew, quietly running the show behind the scenes. Just as you are able to shift your focus to the feeling of your feet on the floor and bring that sensation into your awareness, you can also use language to highlight different aspects of your experiences. In other words, when we ask better questions, we can move the spotlight and discover new information that might have otherwise remained hidden in the shadows.

Typically, when we want to understand another person's motivations, we ask them *why* they feel the way they feel or want what they want. While we might be genuinely curious, the question *why* can often come across as accusatory or even challenging, making the other person feel the need to defend or explain their position. This puts them on the defensive and, by necessity, forces us into an offensive stance, creating a conflict where we end up on opposing sides.

Even if the other person doesn't get defensive, asking *why* usually only brings out surface-level answers which rarely reflect deeper motivations. I mean, let's face it—most of us have no idea *why* we do half the things we do. We're on autopilot much of the time, so nine times out of ten, when you ask someone *why*, you'll just get a shrug and an "I don't know" in response.

Super helpful, right?

The good news is that a simple linguistic shift can change the types of answers we receive. While we can't control what is inside someone else's circle, we can use our language to encourage more meaningful connections.

So, rather than asking *why*, notice what shifts when you ask, '*For what purpose?*' instead.

This small linguistic switch makes a world of difference—I promise.

When you change the question to '*For what purpose*', you invite the other person to unconsciously dig deeper into their motivations—to shine the spotlight on a new part of their internal stage—which can help give you more information on their needs. This shifts the conversation from defending positions to genuinely working to understand each other. While asking '*Why*' can sometimes feel confrontational and triggering, asking '*For what purpose*' tends to reveal something more meaningful about the other person's perspective.

For example, if you ask someone, *why* they want to go to the mall, they might respond with, "I don't know," or give some other vague or unhelpful answer. They might even get defensive and ask, "Why are you asking?"—feeling like they need to justify their desire. This kind of response can stall a conversation and lead to a dead end. However, if you ask them '*For what purpose* do you want to go to the mall?' you're likely to get a much more insightful response.

For instance, they might say they want to find shoes to match a new outfit or check out the new candle store. This not only gives you better insights into their motivations but also helps build a genuine connection.

And that's pretty cool, don't you think?

A few years ago, I worked with a couple who had an explosive disagreement about what type of flooring to install in their kitchen. He wanted grey porcelain tiles, while she preferred vinyl flooring.

HOW TO SET BOUNDARIES WITHOUT FEELING LIKE A D*CK

Initially, their discussions led nowhere because they were each stuck defending their positions. He did everything in his power to convince her that his reasons were better than hers while she did the same. This led to a lot of frustration that was slowly pushing them apart.

Through our coaching work together, they each began shifting their approach from asking *'Why'* to asking *'For what purpose.'*

This simple change made all the difference.

He explained that he wanted the grey porcelain tiles because they were durable and added a modern touch, while she said she preferred vinyl because it was softer underfoot and easier to clean. With this new understanding, they were able to explore new options that met both of their needs. They began to look for a flooring material that combined durability and comfort with a modern look and ease of cleaning, eventually settling on a high-quality laminate that satisfied both of their needs.

This approach transformed what could have been a confrontational exchange into a collaborative exploration; it took them from being on opposite teams to being teammates solving a problem together. By uncovering the underlying motivations behind each other's' desires, they were able to find a creative solution that met both of their needs—without anyone having to compromise.

Now, obviously there were deeper things going on in the relationship, but this one situation became a turning point for both of them. It put them back on the same team and allowed them to collaborate and problem solve together without getting into power struggles. As a result, it began to break down some of the walls they had built up with each other. Conversation by conversation, they learned to ask better questions and, in doing so, built a deeper connection.

This is the essence of compassionate negotiation: understanding the deeper motivations behind what everyone wants and then working together to find a path forward that respects everyone's values and desires.

THE ART OF COMPASSIONATE NEGOTIATION

Let's revisit our door color example from earlier. If we choose compassionate negotiation instead of compromise, the conversation might now go something like this:

Husband: "I want to paint the door black."

Me: "I want to paint it red. For what purpose do you want a black door?"

Husband: "I think a black door looks sophisticated and is easy to maintain. For what purpose do you want a red door?"

Me: "I want something bold and fun that makes a statement.

By asking '*For what purpose,*' we can uncover that I am seeking boldness and fun, while he is looking for sophistication and ease. Now, we can explore options that satisfy both our desires by looking for options that are sophisticated, easy to maintain, bold and fun.

Perhaps a deep purple door could offer the boldness I crave and the sophistication my husband appreciates. Or maybe an elegant navy blue could be a solution that is both fun and easy to maintain.

Compassionate negotiation involves asking better questions and finding creative solutions that neither party might have initially considered. It requires a willingness to explore new possibilities together and an openness to understand each other's motivations and desires.

Learning how to negotiate compassionately can transform even the most volatile conflicts into opportunities for deeper connection and respect. By creating win-win situations, instead of settling for the mutual dissatisfaction often found in compromise, you unlock the true magic of boundaries.

CHAPTER FOURTEEN EXERCISE

Exploring Compassionate Negotiation

When you're in the heat of an argument, it can be hard to remember your new skills. That's why it can be helpful to practice negotiation before you actually need it. Just as you wouldn't wait until someone is on the floor turning blue to learn CPR, it's important to explore conflict resolution and negotiation well ahead of time. In this exercise, the goal is to explore different scenarios where conflict took place and re-imagine them through the lens of compassionate negotiation. All you need is your journal or a notebook and a few moments to yourself. As always, avoid overthinking and just write down the first thing that comes up for you.

Step One: Reflect on a recent conflict

Think back to a disagreement or conflict you had with someone, whether it was recent or from years ago. Imagine yourself back in that moment, seeing it through your own eyes, and note any thoughts or feelings that come up. As you re-live the situation, allow yourself to focus on what you really wanted at that moment—what core need wasn't being met.

Ask yourself, "For what purpose did I want that?" and write down whatever comes to mind.

For example: Let's say you and your spouse disagree about how to spend weekends. You feel like weekends are for running errands, doing household chores, or visiting family, while your spouse wants more downtime at home to relax. If you were to ask, "For what purpose do I want to run errands and do chores on weekends?" you might decide it's to help make the weekdays run more smoothly and to give you more downtime in the evenings.

Step 2: Imagine their needs

Once you've considered the situation from your own perspective, it's time to put yourself in the other person's shoes. Imagine you can see the world through their eyes, experiencing their thoughts and feelings. From this new viewpoint, ask yourself, "For what purpose did they want what they wanted?" Really do your best to understand where they're coming from—remember, the goal is to use the conversation as a bridge to a deeper connection. You can't do that without considering their side of things. In this step, your job is to imagine their motivations, feelings, and any external pressures they might have been facing.

For example: If you were to ask, "For what purpose does my partner want to stay home and relax on weekends?" you might decide it's to help feel more prepared and rested for the week ahead and to get some time to recharge.

Remember that every behavior has a positive underlying intention and this isn't about agreeing with anyone; it's about trying to understand a fellow human being. While you can never truly know what's going on in someone else's head, you can make an educated guess for the purpose of helping you develop and refine your compassionate negotiation skills.

Step 3: Find common ground

Once you've explored both sides of the story, it's time to compare the two and find a common thread, no matter how small. To do this, imagine viewing your relationship from a bird's-eye view perspective. If it helps, you can imagine yourself as a wise owl or majestic eagle flying overhead, looking down on both you and the other person. From this neutral vantage point, notice what you both have in common and jot down your observations. What is something you both want?

For example: Both you and your partner want to help make the upcoming week easier and have more downtime to recharge.

Step 4: Come up with some new solutions

Once you've identified even the smallest thread of common ground, it's time to brainstorm possible solutions that address the shared need or interest. In this step, see if you can come up with some creative options and then jot down 2-3 that could potentially solve the problem and allow both you and the other person to get your needs met based on the common thread you just discovered.

For example: One way to make the upcoming week easier and have more downtime might include designating one weekend day for errands and chores and the other day for relaxation or doing something fun together, ensuring a balance between productivity and relaxation. It might involve creating a weekly schedule that includes time slots for errands, chores, and relaxation, allowing both of you to feel more in control and less overwhelmed. Or perhaps even alternating weekends where one weekend is dedicated to family visits and social activities, while the next is reserved for downtime at home, giving each person a chance to recharge in their preferred way. These options offer a way to acknowledge both of your needs, making it a true win-win scenario.

Step 5: Reflect

Take a moment to return to your own perspective and recall the situation again through your own eyes. Reflect on how you feel about the conflict now, noticing what has shifted and if anything has changed for you. Write your observations down in your journal.

Feel free to repeat this exercise for any relationship, situation or conflict where you'd like a fresh perspective. The more you practice, the easier and more natural it will feel in the moment.

Final Thoughts:

Remember, this exercise is about imagining a conversation for the purpose of practicing the art of compassionate negotiation. The goal isn't to single-handedly fix a relationship but to build and refine your own skills for real-life situations.

This exercise can help you develop more flexibility in your thinking so you can become more comfortable asking different questions. If going through all the steps feels too overwhelming, you can start by simply replacing the question "*Why*" with "*For what purpose*" in your everyday conversations.

THE ART OF COMPASSIONATE NEGOTIATION

For example, if a friend says they want to order take-out, ask, "For what purpose?" If your kids want to watch a certain movie, ask, "For what purpose?" This approach lets you practice using different language without triggering defensive reactions or causing anyone to shut down. You might even learn something new about them.

However, be mindful not to overdo it. Excessive questioning—even when using better language—can still infringe on others' boundaries and may lead to frustration or anger.

CHAPTER FIFTEEN
Offering Compassionate Feedback

"Feedback is a gift that lights the path towards growth." -Unknown

Well, you did it! You spoke up, shared your boundary, used the Boundaries Blueprint formula, and voiced your desires in a way that opened a space for negotiation, collaboration and connection.

Woo-hoo!

And then the other person went and trampled all over the boundary you just set.

F#@k!!!! Now what??

Having someone ignore the boundary you worked so hard to share can feel invalidating and infuriating, but I want to assure you that this is a normal part of the boundary-setting process.

In this chapter, I want to go deeper into the idea of having our boundaries tested and introduce you to a powerful resource—the Feedback Formula. This linguistic tool will help you offer better support and guidance as someone adjusts to respecting your new boundaries.

Because here's the thing about your boundaries: they are yours. And while they are extremely obvious and important to you, they are likely just one of the many conversations the other person had that day. So it makes sense that they might not get your message on the first try. And that's okay. In fact, it's pretty much a requirement based on how our brains operate.

Testing boundaries is a necessary part of the learning process, which is why knowing how to offer compassionate feedback is another essential skill on your boundary-setting journey.

Why Repetition Matters

In addition to being a competent processor of sensory data, the human brain is also a remarkable pattern-seeking machine that constantly scans the environment for familiar shapes and sequences. This is part of why we can see faces in the clouds and constellations in the stars. Our brains are designed to prioritize information based on patterns because identifying patterns is a big part of how our neurology learns. When something happens once or twice, our brains tend to dismiss or ignore it, assuming it is simply an anomaly or a coincidence. In fact, our brains really only begin to pay attention to something when it is either highly emotionally-charged and traumatic, or when it is part of a larger pattern. Outside of these scenarios, it doesn't invest much processing power.

This means, the first time you share your boundary with someone, their brain might not prioritize the information right away, and they may even completely forget your boundary altogether.

Is it infuriating? Yes.

Is it normal? Also yes!

To help understand this better, let me share a story about my cousin's neighbor, Sarah.

Sarah lived just on the outskirts of town on a large, open lot with lots and lots of space and no fences. Her dog, Max, a beautiful border collie, was the king of this outdoor domain and would roam freely, chasing squirrels and taking naps in the sunshine, always perfectly safe and content. One day, the peace of Max's outdoor sanctuary was

HOW TO SET BOUNDARIES WITHOUT FEELING LIKE A D*CK

rudely disrupted by the arrival of a construction company, marking the start of a new housing development that was being built right at the edge of Sarah's property. As the construction workers began to dig trenches and lay foundations, Max's once-open playground became a hub of activity and noise.

Concerned for Max's safety, Sarah knew she could no longer let Max wander freely, but tethering him on a leash seemed cruel since he was used to total freedom. She was determined to find a solution that would keep Max safe, while still preserving his ability to roam, and finally decided to invest in something called an *invisible fence*—a boundary that would be felt but not seen. If you have never heard of them before, an invisible fence works by emitting a signal along a buried wire, creating an invisible perimeter that, when crossed, triggers a warning or mild correction (like a noise or a vibration) for the dog who is wearing a special collar.

When the invisible fence was first installed, Max was completely oblivious because, from his perspective, nothing had changed. He had no reason to suspect anything was different and so he bounded around his yard like he always did—until he encountered the invisible boundary and received a signal on his collar.

At first, Max barely paused, brushing off the unfamiliar sensation as a minor inconvenience and continuing to run around as he had always done before. But as Max continued to encounter the invisible boundary, he began to notice that something was different. According to Sarah, the next few times he approached the border, instead of running past the line as if nothing was different, he ran through it then paused briefly, turning around to investigate the area before bouncing off again. He clearly noticed something was different but likely didn't know what it was yet.

It wasn't until the fourth or fifth encounter with the new invisible fence line that Max really began to notice that something new was there; a boundary had been created. As he neared the border, he now started to slow to a walk and sniff the area, trying to identify this new thing that had appeared where once there was nothing. Sarah said she could almost see him testing the limits of this newfound border. After a few more encounters, Max seemed to understand that this new boundary was there to stay and, aside from a few squirrel-chasing incidents, has stayed happily and safely within his newly defined yard.

Like Max, the people in your life may need repeated reminders and experiences to fully understand and respect the boundaries that you share. It doesn't mean they are trying to hurt you or that they don't care about you. It simply means their brain is learning something new.

How Your Brain Learns

While there's a wealth of information available about how our brains learn, my personal favorite is based on the four stages of learning first introduced by educational psychologist Noel Burch in the 1970s. This model, often called the *Conscious Competence Model*, describes the process we go through anytime we acquire new skills or knowledge.[22] As it turns out, understanding this can also make sharing your boundaries much easier—and, frankly, less dramatic. So, let's go through them one by one:

Stage 1: Unconscious Incompetence—You don't know what you don't know

In this stage of the learning process, we are blissfully unaware of our lack of skill or knowledge in a particular area and likely don't even recognize that there's room for improvement. We are oblivious to the fact that there's a problem or something we need to learn because we don't know what we don't know. This stage can feel very comfortable because ignorance is bliss—and it's also the first step on the journey toward learning something new.

For our friend, Max the dog, before encountering the invisible fence, he was completely unaware of any need for boundaries or limitations in his backyard. He roamed freely, blissfully unaware of the potential dangers lurking beyond.

Stage 2: Conscious Incompetence—You know what you don't know

At this stage, we have now become aware of our lack of skill or knowledge in a certain area, and we can begin to recognize the need for improvement or change—but we may still feel a sense of confusion or inadequacy as we begin the learning process. Here, we are actively working to develop new competence and skills because we now understand what we didn't know before, and we are eager to fix it.

Motivation tends to be quite high during this stage because we are driven to find answers and solutions to the problems we've just identified. This newfound awareness fuels our determination to improve and grow.

With little Max, when the invisible fence was first installed, he encountered the boundary but didn't fully understand its significance yet. He received a warning, signaling that he had crossed a line, but the concept of the boundary hadn't fully registered. There was an awareness, but also a complete and total lack of comprehension and understanding.

Stage 3: Conscious Competence—You Know What You Know

In this stage, we've acquired the necessary skills or knowledge we need to move forward, but we still have to consciously focus on what we're doing to perform correctly. Think of a new driver who has passed the written exam and driving test but still remains hyper-aware of every action behind the wheel. While they can drive competently, it still requires a fair amount of conscious effort and concentration—it hasn't yet become a fully automatic habit.

At this stage of learning, we know what we need to do—and we're doing it! But it still feels a bit awkward, unnatural and unfamiliar. Patience and repetition are key here as this is often when feelings of frustration and impatience can start to surface.

During this phase of learning, there's a lot of testing of new boundaries and skills as we attempt to fully understand and integrate them into our lives and existing habits.

With our canine friend, Max, the more times he encountered the invisible boundary, the more he understood its significance. Over time, he learned to recognize the warning signals and adjust his behavior to stay within the new boundaries.

OFFERING COMPASSIONATE FEEDBACK

Stage 4: Unconscious Competence—You don't know what you know

Finally, in this stage, we have mastered the new skill to the point where it becomes second nature to us, and we can perform it effortlessly, without much conscious thought. It has become ingrained in our behavior and is executed almost instinctively—like we are on auto-pilot.

For Max, repeated encounters with the invisible fence allowed his neurology to internalize the concept of the boundary, and respecting the invisible fence became second nature to him.

It became an ingrained behavior—a new habit.

You might be thinking, this is all well and good, but what does all this have to do with boundaries? What many of us tend to forget when we share our boundaries for the first time is that we are, in essence, training another person to respect something they didn't initially recognize as a problem. Sharing your boundaries is a learning process for both you and the other person. This means that, despite feeling impatient, you will both need to move through all four learning stages as you integrate this new boundary into your relationship.

This is where feedback becomes vitally important.

Knowing how to offer compassionate and effective feedback is a beautiful gift. It allows you to encourage and support a fellow human being as they learn something new—your boundary—so you can honor your own desires and wishes without having to resort to being 'Nice.'

Unfortunately, most of us are not taught how to give healthy, effective, and compassionate feedback. Instead, we are taught to offer *constructive criticism*. Yuck.

The Pitfalls of Constructive Criticism

Criticism, regardless of intent, is still criticism. It involves pointing out what someone did wrong, or failed to do, and there's no scenario in which that will ever feel genuinely safe or supportive.

Think about the last time someone offered you constructive criticism. Did it feel good and did you accept it easily? Or did it make you feel inadequate and defensive—even if you didn't show it?

Most likely, it was the latter.

Even well-meaning criticism has the capacity to trigger a person's fight-flight-freeze response and, when this happens, instead of actually considering the feedback, the recipient is more likely to become defensive, withdraw, or shut down completely. Even when we logically know it's meant to be helpful, constructive criticism can still trigger feelings of hurt, shame, or anger, leading to rejection of the feedback and resentment of the person delivering it. Which means not only is constructive criticism hurtful, it's also completely ineffective.

Feedback, unlike constructive criticism, is a gift. It is a beautiful opportunity that allows you to share openly and honestly, without worrying about either person being triggered. And much like the Boundaries Blueprint, offering compassionate feedback works best when you follow a simple linguistic formula which I like to call the *Feedback Formula*.

The Feedback Formula:

The concept of effective feedback was first popularized by management and leadership expert, Ken Blanchard, in his book *The One Minute Manager*, which was first published in 1982.[23] In the book, Blanchard introduces the concept of sandwiching constructive criticism between two layers of positive feedback as a way to offer input effectively while maintain motivation and morale.

While I love the basic structure of this model, it stills requires the use of "constructive criticism" which, as we just learned, also comes with the risk of triggering the other person into a fight, flight or freeze response. Luckily, with just a few linguistic shifts, we can easily transform this concept into an easy-to-use formula that maintains a space of compassion, while also allowing both you and the other person to feel safe and appreciated.

OFFERING COMPASSIONATE FEEDBACK

By following this formula, you can create a clear and supportive three-part feedback message to share with the other person, which not only helps in reinforcing your boundary but also encourages a healthy and respectful dialogue.

Let's go through this step-by-step.

(1) Share Something You Loved:

To begin, start with the words "I love(d)..." and then share something you genuinely love or appreciate about the other person as it relates to what you are giving feedback on. Just like in the Boundaries Blueprint, the key here is sincerity. If you make something up just to be '*Nice*', the other person will sense it and it will undermine the feedback you are offering.

Here are some examples:

"I loved the enthusiasm you brought to the project. Your energy was contagious and really kept the team motivated."

"I love how much thought you put into your presentation. It was evident that you took the time to research and prepare."

"I love that you caught yourself yelling and changed to a gentler tone."

"I love that you called to let me know your plans for the weekend."

(2) Share What You Would Love More/Less Of:

Next, use the words "I would love more/less..." and this time, share what you would love to see more or less of as it relates to the other person's behavior or performance. This step helps to communicate your needs clearly without making it sound like a demand.

Examples include:

"I would love to see more focus in your work. I noticed a few areas where things seemed a bit scattered, and I think honing in on specific tasks could help streamline the process."

"I would love less hesitation when it comes to sharing your ideas during meetings. Your insights are valuable, and I believe speaking up more could greatly benefit the team."

"I would love to hear less accusations and blaming when we are talking about something important."

"I would love more communication about your specific plans so I know where you'll be and who you'll be with."

(3) Share What You Loved Overall:

Conclude with the words "Overall, I loved..." and then genuinely share what you loved or appreciated from a more general perspective. This approach helps highlight the positives and leaves the conversation on a high note, making the other person feel valued and encouraged.

For example:

"Overall, I loved your dedication and commitment to getting your homework done on time. Your hard work hasn't gone unnoticed, and I'm excited to see where you can go from here."

"Overall, I love having you on our team. Your positive attitude and willingness to tackle challenges head-on make you a valuable asset, and I'm looking forward to seeing your continued growth."

"Overall, I love how committed you are to communicating your needs more compassionately with me."

"Overall, I love that you are keeping me in the loop and sharing your schedule with me."

Feedback and Boundaries

So how does this work when it comes to boundaries? Let's say you share a boundary using the Boundaries Blueprint that goes something like this:

"I appreciate you are upset and angry right now and I would love to be spoken to in a more respectful tone."

OFFERING COMPASSIONATE FEEDBACK

And then, sometime later, you find yourself in the same situation, being yelled at by the same person you already shared your boundary with.

Now what?

For many of us, this is where we might abandon our shiny new boundary and either shut down the conversation or put up a Wall (conditions), trying to force the other person to change their behavior with threats of punishment or abandonment. We might get upset and say, "I told you not to yell at me; obviously, you don't respect me or my boundaries. If you don't stop yelling, I'm going to walk out the door."

The good news is, you'll likely feel empowered for having spoken up! The not-so-great news is that by handling it this way, you miss an opportunity for genuine connection. As a result, neither of you gets your needs fully met.

How sad.

Now, notice what shifts when we use the Feedback Formula instead.

Using the example above, you might offer the following feedback: "I love how passionate you are about this. I would love to hear less shouting and more respect. Overall, I'm really glad we're talking about this." This approach allows the other person to feel respected while still upholding and valuing your initial boundary; it allows you to feel heard without having to resort to tactics that negate connection or escalate the conversation into a full-blown fight or confrontation.

Remember, the other person will typically test your boundary multiple times—usually at least three—as they navigate the stages of learning and their brain adjusts to the new behavior you're requesting. If you give up after the first test, you risk feeling like a victim of their behavior and missing out on the chance to build the authenticity and connection that comes from navigating these uncomfortable conversations together.

Will speaking this way feel awkward? Absolutely!

Will it still work? You betcha.

Keep in mind, as you embark on this boundary-setting journey, you will also be navigating the four stages of learning. Integrating these new skills and formulas into your life is going to feel strange and awkward at first, but that simply means you've reached the third stage of learning, and you're only one step away from making it a new and permanent habit. And that's exciting!

So take a hefty dose of vitamin P—*patience*—and keep practicing with as much consistency as possible, knowing that perfection is never the goal. Before you know it, you'll be easily sharing your boundaries and nurturing them with effective feedback that fosters compassion and deep connection.

No criticism—constructive or otherwise—required.

A Recap Of The Feedback Formula:

1. Share what you loved by using the phrase:

"I love(d)..."

2. Share what you would love to see more or less of by using the phrase:

"I would love to see more/less..."

3. Finally, share what you appreciated overall by using the phrase:

"Overall, I love..."

OFFERING COMPASSIONATE FEEDBACK

HOW TO SET BOUNDARIES WITHOUT FEELING LIKE A D*CK

CHAPTER FIFTEEN ACTIVITY
Becoming a Feedback Fan

The key to successful boundary-setting isn't just about defining your boundaries, but also preparing for potential reactions and offering compassionate feedback in response. This exercise is designed to help you identify situations where others may challenge or disregard your boundaries to give you the opportunity to share your guidance and feedback.

In this activity, you will imagine some of the possible reactions you may have to the boundaries you identified and wrote out a few chapters ago.

As always, all you need for this exercise is a pen, your journal or a notebook and a few moments to yourself.

Start by creating a chart like the one below:

Boundary Crossed	What Went Right	What You Want More/Less Of	Overall, What You Want

Step One: Write your crossed boundaries

In the first column, list the boundaries you have tried to set in the past that have been crossed or haven't quite stuck.

For example, maybe you asked for more help around the house but your partner continues to leave dishes by the sink.

Step Two: Explore what went right

In the next column, take a moment to reflect on what is going well. Even if the boundary was crossed, consider any positive efforts the other person has made in other areas by zooming out and looking at the bigger picture.

For example, if your partner forgot to do a chore you asked them to, they might have shown appreciation in other ways, like making an effort to spend quality time with you or surprising you with a small gesture of kindness.

Step Three: Get clear on what you want more or less of in the future

In the third column, write down what you want more or less of regarding the other person's behavior. Be specific about the changes you'd like to see. For example, you might want less ignoring the dishes and more help cleaning up after dinner.

Step Four: Express what you loved overall

Finally, in the last column, reflect on what you appreciate about the other person and your relationship as a whole. This helps to frame your feedback in a compassionate way.

By focusing on the positives, you create a more balanced perspective, which can make it easier to approach difficult conversations with understanding and kindness.

For example, you might appreciate that you have a partner who is open to hearing what you have to say.

Boundary Crossed	What Went Right	What You Want More/Less Of	Overall, What You Want
I want help around the house and dishes not left in the sink overnight	Gave me a nice back and foot rub before bed	More doing the dishes, less leaving them until the morning	I love that we can talk about this stuff

Once you have completed these steps, simply weave them together to create your feedback:

"I love that you gave me a nice back and foot rub before bed. I would love more doing the dishes and less leaving them until the morning. Overall, I really love that we can talk about this stuff."

Remember that every boundary will be tested multiple times as the other person goes through the four stages of learning. That's why learning to offer compassionate feedback is an essential skill for any boundary-setting warrior. Knowing how to offer patience and understanding during these moments of growth helps to reinforce your boundary while also fostering mutual respect and connection.

By taking a few minutes to reflect and write down your thoughts in this format, you'll find it easier to communicate your feedback when the time comes.

Troubleshooting:

If despite consistently and clearly use of the Boundaries Blueprint and Feedback Formula, your boundaries are still disregarded, it may signal deeper relationship issues. Seeking support from a relationship coach, counselor, or therapist can provide valuable guidance and resources. If you suspect you could use some assistance in this area of your life, I encourage to you seek out support.

OFFERING COMPASSIONATE FEEDBACK

CHAPTER SIXTEEN

The Flipside of Boundaries: Receptivity

"Receptivity is the soil in which the seeds of wisdom grow."
- Unknown

Now that we have thoroughly explored the importance of setting and honoring healthy boundaries, negotiating shared space, and offering compassionate feedback, it's time to dive into the flipside of boundaries: Receptivity.

In this chapter, I want to focus on this often overlooked but important aspect of healthy boundaries.

Up to this point, our journey has focused on using boundaries to know ourselves better, keep out what we don't want, and to clarify what we do want. But, once we've created that space and asked for what we desire, we need to make sure we are open and ready to receive what shows up.

Otherwise, what's the point, right?

Receptivity is not some lovey-dovey, New Age concept—it is a fundamental skill that many of us have neglected because we have been taught that it's unimportant, and that it is better to give than to receive. While giving is wonderful, failing to balance it with receptivity can lead to a life where we give and give and give but have no idea what to do when something good actually comes our way. Without knowing how to be receptive, the person of our dreams could literally show up on our doorstep holding buckets of money and all the answers to our prayers and we would still find a way to somehow dismiss, invalidate, or reject it.

Even worse, when we continuously reject the kindness and positive things that come our way, we can start to perpetuate the false idea that we're not worthy of good things.

Yikes.

It's no surprise that so many of us end up feeling invisible and undervalued.

Boundaries Work Both Ways

Think of your boundaries as a two-way street. While, yes, they keep out negativity and protect you from getting hurt, they also create a space for good things to come into your life—like compliments, affection, love, and support. Learning how to receive these things graciously into your life is an essential part of setting healthy boundaries and is key for developing a strong sense of self-worth.

Back in my early 20s, I loved to go out dancing with friends at clubs, but whenever we went out, I noticed people would line up to offer my friends compliments and drinks, while I often felt invisible, wondering why no one approached me. It often made me feel less attractive and interesting than my friends.

Looking back, I realize I was actually the one creating that situation by not knowing how to receive graciously. Whenever a cute guy would make eye contact with me, I would quickly look away, too shy or unsure to hold his gaze. If someone was brave enough to approach me and offer me a compliment, my go-to response was something flippant like, "Wow, you must be really drunk if you think I'm pretty." They'd walk away feeling rejected, and I'd continue to wonder why I was still alone.

The problem wasn't that I was less attractive or interesting—it was that I didn't know how to accept the compliments and attention graciously. My awkward responses and dismissive attitude were likely off-putting, making it hard for others to connect with me. Learning to receive graciously could have made a huge difference, not just in how others saw me but also in how I felt about myself.

The Gift of Receptivity

In many cultures, there is often an over-emphasis on being giving and generous. From a young age, we are taught that giving is noble and virtuous—which is absolutely true. However, learning to receive the good things that are offered to us is just as important and creates a foundation for gratitude to grow. Scientific research shows that being open to love, kindness, and support has a profound impact on our brains and our relationships. It increases oxytocin, the "love hormone," which builds trust, strengthens bonds, and reduces stress.[24] It also activates mirror neurons, specialized cells in the brain that are associated with connection and empathy.

Psychologically, being more receptive helps us form secure attachments, improves communication, and makes us more empathetic listeners. It also promotes better conflict resolution by fostering mutual understanding and cooperation. Just as being receptive enhances our personal growth and relationships, it also benefits those around us. By allowing others to give to us, we create space for mutual appreciation and connection.

Think about the last time you gave someone a gift or did something kind for them. The real joy in offering kindness comes from seeing the other person's reaction, right? It is in witnessing their gratitude and appreciation that makes our efforts feel worthwhile and rewarding. When someone smiles, says thank you, or expresses how much your gesture means to them, it creates a bond. When our kindness is acknowledged, we feel valued.

Many of us mistakenly believe that being humble means rejecting or brushing off the kindness and good things offered to us. For example, when someone gives us a gift, we might say, "Oh, you shouldn't have." Or when we get a compliment, we respond with the

THE FLIPSIDE OF BOUNDARIES: RECEPTIVITY

standard, "Oh, this old thing?" We get so used to brushing off good things that we don't even realize how much we're holding ourselves back from enjoying all the positivity life has to offer.

When we don't know how to receive graciously, it can be hard to feel truly happy about our accomplishments, even if we've worked really hard for them, and it can leave us feeling never quite satisfied with our life. Moreover, the inability to be receptive can put a major strain on our relationships.

Imagine giving a gift to a friend, only to have it brushed aside or rejected. It would feel disheartening and likely make you hesitant to offer them a gift again in the future. When we dismiss or downplay acts of kindness, we not only miss out on feeling loved and appreciated, we also unintentionally send the message that the other person's efforts don't matter.

Years ago, a good friend of mine went through a rough patch in her marriage. According to her, one of the problems was that her partner had stopped doing nice things for her. Sure, there were still flowers once a year and cards on holidays, but all the wonderful romantic gestures that had made their dating period so special had faded away. My friend admitted that while she loved all the romantic gestures from the early days, she always felt super awkward accepting them. Instead of graciously receiving these acts of love, she would often make a joke or downplay how much they meant to her. She thought it was just a bit of harmless self-deprecating humor or modesty, but over time, the loving gestures stopped.

During one of their couples counseling sessions, her partner shared that the off-hand comments and dismissals had made them feel rejected and unappreciated. They admitted that this was why they had given up on the romantic gestures—they felt their efforts were not valued.

When we struggle to receive—whether due to feelings of unworthiness, pride, or discomfort—we unintentionally deprive others of the joy that comes from giving. While we might think we're being clever by hiding our discomfort with humor or sarcasm, this can unintentionally invalidate the other person's genuine effort to connect, which can feel quite hurtful.

The Importance of Influence

Being more receptive isn't just about accepting compliments, feedback, or a drink from someone at a bar. It's also about letting yourself be influenced by others and being willing to consider their ideas and viewpoints. This is another fundamental yet often overlooked aspect of building and maintaining healthy boundaries.

According to John Gottman, a renowned psychologist and researcher in the field of marriage and relationships, learning to be receptive to the influence of others is actually critical for relationship success. In fact, in relationships where one partner is not willing to accept the influence of their significant other, they are up to 81% more likely to end in divorce[25].

Being receptive goes beyond just saying "Thank you" more graciously. It involves being open to the thoughts, feelings, and experiences of those around you. It's about genuinely considering their opinions, ideas, and desires while still honoring and valuing your own.

Years ago, I heard a quote that has always stuck with me: "If you both love the sunrise, how will you ever get to experience a sunset?" By stepping outside our usual preferences and allowing ourselves to be positively influenced by other people, we allow ourselves, and the relationship, to grow in unexpected and beautiful ways.

This is the healing power of healthy boundaries.

Healthy boundaries are what allow us to safely consider different perspectives and adjust our behavior to fit—without losing ourselves in the process. They enable us to be positively influenced by others while still honoring our own playbook and staying true to *Who We Are*. It is this beautiful and intricate dance that allows us to create relationships that are more balanced, and ultimately, more fulfilling.

So, what are some things you are meant to be able to receive into your life?

- Compliments
- Help

- Support
- Kindness
- Love
- Opportunities
- Feedback
- Gifts
- Kudos
- Time
- Attention
- Affection
- Forgiveness
- Advice
- Rest
- Relaxation
- Joy
- Happiness
- Inspiration
- Peace
- Trust

Being Graciously Awkward

If you're anything like me, you're probably thinking, "Sure, this all sounds great, but how do I do this without feeling totally awkward?"

I get it! I've been there.

Learning to receive did not come naturally to me. Growing up in my family, accepting kindness often felt like painting a target on my back for ridicule or judgment, so I mastered the art of deflection just to feel safe in an environment that often wasn't. But here's what I've learned since: the coping mechanisms that helped me survive in chaos are useless when it comes to building healthy, empowering, and fulfilling relationships.

Like all new skills, the journey to becoming more receptive takes practice, patience, and a whole lot of self-compassion. And for some of us, it may always feel a little strange. In fact, I'll let you in on a little secret: I still feel ridiculously awkward when someone gives me a gift or compliment. Every. Single. Time. I have just learned not to let that awkwardness stop me.

To be honest, I'd rather awkwardly accept the gifts and kindness the world offers me than push them away and wonder why life feels so empty. Embracing the awkwardness is just part of the journey sometimes, and leaning into the discomfort can be a powerful reminder that you're breaking old patterns and creating new ones that better serve the life you want to build.

So yeah—it's totally okay to feel a little awkward at first.

Using Humor to Embrace Receptivity

If you still find yourself feeling weird about compliments, despite your best efforts to be more receptive, you're not alone. It can be tough to break the habit of deflecting kindness. Which is why I want to introduce you to what I call the "*Yeah, I'm the shit*" technique.

Before you raise an eyebrow or dismiss this idea as too bold, let me explain.

Using a bit of humor and irreverence when accepting compliments can actually turn our defensive reactions into something positive. Rather than deflecting a compliment with a clever remark, we can use that same humor to get more comfortable with receiving praise. Being playful can make it easier to accept kind words from others because it taps into something we all have: a sense of humor.

Years ago, a good friend of mine taught me the "*Yeah, I'm the shit*" technique after I had been complaining to her that no one ever hit on me in bars. In fact, she was the one who first suggested that it might be because I didn't know how to take a compliment. When I complained that it was just too awkward and I never knew what to say she told me, "Do what I do – just look them dead in the eye and say 'Yeah, I'm the shit.'"

Initially, I thought she was out of her mind. I was like, "There is no way I can pull that off." It felt way too bold for my tastes. But my friend assured me it worked and that it helped her get over her fear of accepting compliments.

That next Saturday night, we went out dancing, and once again I was left on my own while my friend received lots of attention. It wasn't that no one was interested in me—plenty of people came up to compliment me on one thing or another. But every time, I felt weird and awkward, so I'd use humor to make them go away.

After watching my friend, I decided it was time to try her approach. When the next person came up and complimented me, instead of brushing it off or making a flippant remark, I looked them straight in the eye and said, "Yeah, I'm the shit." And you know what? It totally worked! No one was more surprised than me when they smiled, and we ended up having a great conversation. It was such a small and silly little thing, but it seriously made all the difference in how the rest of the night played out. I have since taught this approach to many of my friends and clients and each of them have had the same experience as me. It turns out, instead of using sarcasm to push people away, we can use irreverence to create a connection.

Who knew it could be so easy!

Since then, it's become my go-to method for accepting compliments when I don't know what else to say. I've used this phrase in various settings, from my friend's backyard BBQ to corporate meetings and even once on stage. This fun technique has not only helped me gradually get used to accepting compliments but has also boosted my confidence. Plus, it almost always brings a smile to the other person's face and is a great way to open a conversation.

Learning to Cultivate Grace

Not quite ready for the boldness of saying, "Yeah, I'm the shit," but still want to improve your ability to receive compliments? Try this simple technique: the next time someone offers you a gift or a compliment, place your hand over your heart and say, "Received" or "I appreciate that."

This small, mindful gesture can make a big difference in how you cultivate gratitude and receptivity in your life.

Final Thoughts

Being more receptive is about more than just saying "thank you" when someone is kind to you. It's about genuinely allowing good things to come your way without pushing them away or shutting them down.

The more you practice being receptive, the more you invite new opportunities and possibilities into your life. This is how you use your boundaries to create a space for magic to enter into your life.

THE FLIPSIDE OF BOUNDARIES: RECEPTIVITY

CHAPTER SIXTEEN ACTIVITY
The "I Would Love" Exercise

As you'll recall, your desires are anything that you really, truly want in any given moment or situation. They can range from your biggest dreams to your smallest wishes and they are reflections of the most authentic parts of *Who You Are*. Which means, if your goal is to be more receptive, the first step is to get more comfortable declaring what it is that you want.

Most of us are conditioned to talk about our desires using phrases like "I need to" or "I should," which linguistically turns them into items on a to-do list. For example, instead of saying "I want to get my car washed," we might say "I need to get my car washed." This can unintentionally push what we want to the bottom of a long list of obligations.

Changing the language to "I would love," however, can keep our desires front and center and allows us to honor them without turning them into chores. This small linguistic shift can create a powerful change in our ability to be more receptive.

In this activity, the goal is to get comfortable expressing your desires by using the phrase "I would love" as often as possible throughout the day. This practice is designed to help you become more attuned to what you want and open the door to being more receptive to what life has to offer.

Step One: Share your desires with abandon

Throughout the day, as often as you can remember, use the phrase "I would love..." to express something you want. Whether it's a simple craving for a cup of coffee or a big dream about your perfect vacation, let yourself acknowledge your desires. It could even be something totally fantastical like a teleportation device or a pet unicorn. The goal is to get comfortable identifying what you want, no matter how insignificant or kooky it may be.

Here's the key: you must say your desires OUT LOUD—even if no one else is around to hear you. Speaking your desires into existence is a powerful act that takes what's inside you—your dreams and desires—and brings it into the world through the sound of your voice. Saying "I would love" might feel like a small gesture, but I promise, it has a big impact. By speaking your desires out loud, you're no longer keeping them locked in your head—you're giving them space to exist in the world.

The simple yet powerful act of voicing what you want sends a strong message to yourself and to the world: your desires matter, and so do you.

Step Two: Reflect and celebrate

At the end of the day, take a few moments to reflect on your experience. Notice any shifts in your awareness or mindset as a result of vocalizing your desires and celebrate your courage and willingness to embrace what you want openly and unapologetically.

Some More Inspiration

Still need help attuning to what you would love? Here are some examples to guide and inspire you. Use these as a starting point for your own "I would love..." declarations and tailor them to fit your unique desires and circumstances.

At Work:

- "I would love to take on a leadership role in our next project."
- "I would love to have a brainstorming session with the team to generate new ideas."
- "I would love to receive more feedback on my performance to help me grow."

With Family:

- "I would love to spend more quality time together on weekends."

- "I would love to plan a family vacation to the beach this year."
- "I would love to start a new tradition of family game night once a week."

With Friends:

- "I would love to host a game night at my place this weekend."
- "I would love to try that new restaurant with you guys sometime soon."
- "I would love to go on a weekend getaway trip with our group."

Personal Growth:

- "I would love to learn a new language this year."
- "I would love to take a cooking class to expand my culinary skills."
- "I would love to read more books and set a goal of one book per month."

Health and Wellness:

- "I would love to start a daily meditation practice."
- "I would love to join a local gym and commit to regular workouts."
- "I would love to adopt a healthier diet and try cooking new recipes."

Hobbies and Interests:

- "I would love to take up painting as a creative outlet."
- "I would love to join a book club to discuss my favorite reads with others."
- "I would love to learn how to play a musical instrument, like the guitar."

THE FLIPSIDE OF BOUNDARIES: RECEPTIVITY

CHAPTER SEVENTEEN

When Sh*t Goes Sideways

"Obstacles are the universe's gentle way of rerouting you and guiding you to your true path."- Unknown

As you have seen, embarking on a journey to establish and maintain healthy boundaries is a profound act of healing and self-discovery that has the power to transform every aspect of your life. By choosing this path, you have taken a courageous step toward finding your authentic voice and have begun the process of rewriting your story and honoring *Who You Are* in a deep and meaningful way.

As you continue to integrate these new tools and concepts into your life, you will naturally begin to expand your comfort zone and, as you do, create new boundaries with the world around you. And, just like all boundaries, these new limits will also need to be tested.

In this chapter, I want to explore what happens when obstacles naturally begin to show up on your path. While unexpected challenges can make us feel like we have taken a step backward or are doing something wrong, it's important to understand that these perceived setbacks are actually a normal and necessary part of the boundary-setting process.

The Science of Setbacks

Have you ever noticed that just when it feels like you're finally starting to make progress toward your goals, something happens that derails your entire plan? Maybe an unexpected expense shows up, siphoning funds away from your dream vacation, or your car breaks down, leaving you stranded and unable to get to work.

Why does it always seem like just when we're finally starting to hit our stride, something happens that knocks us off course?

Ugh.

While it might feel like the universe is conspiring against us, these seemingly random obstacles are actually just a natural part of how our brains handle change.

Our habits are controlled by a part of the brain known as the *basal ganglia*, which are deep neurological structures responsible for managing movement, routines, and decision-making.[26] The basal ganglia help transform our repetitive actions into automatic habits, so we don't have to constantly think about every little thing that we do. While this helps reduce our mental load, it can, unfortunately, make breaking a habit, changing our routine, or moving beyond the limits of our comfort zone a little tricky.

In his book *The Power of Habit: Why We Do What We Do in Life and Business*, Pulitzer Prize-winning journalist Charles Duhigg explains that any time we try to change our routines, it creates something called cognitive dissonance, a feeling of discomfort that results when our actions are not in alignment with what our neurology is used to.[27] In response, our unconscious mind starts looking for ways to pull us back inside our comfort zone to ease the tension.

Think of it like your car's GPS system. When you're following a familiar route, everything runs smoothly. But the moment you take an unexpected turn, your GPS immediately alerts you and recalculates to get you back on track. In the same way, as you start setting new boundaries and stepping outside your comfort zone, your brain's warning system will inevitably kick in and start sending signals designed to redirect you back to what feels safe and familiar. When this happens, you might find yourself facing unexpected scheduling conflicts, relationship tensions, child care hiccups, technological glitches, or even minor health issues.

Remember that your neurology is processing nearly 11 million bits of information every single second. To help manage that massive influx of data, our brains have evolved to filter out anything new or unfamiliar, instead continuously shifting our awareness back to what feels familiar and known. This natural filtering process is critical for our survival, but it can also cause our brains to cling to old habits and routines, making it difficult to change them—even when it's in our best interest.

Since anything outside our comfort zone is unfamiliar—and therefore unknown and potentially threatening to our neurology—any time we start to move beyond the edge of what feels familiar, our unconscious mind will begin projecting our doubts, worries, and fears onto the people and situations around us in an effort to distract us and pull us back into the safety of what we already know. And, much like everything else in nature, our minds will always seek the path of least resistance. So, if an argument with your partner usually works to make you abandon your goals and retreat into the safety of your comfort zone, expect that pattern to resurface. Or if unexpected disruptions—like a sick child, a family emergency, or a crazy work schedule—often make you think, "Maybe now's not the right time," those situations are likely to come up again.

These familiar scenarios are your mind's way of recalculating your route to bring you back to what's known and predictable. Luckily, once you recognize what's going on, you can start to see these challenges and setbacks as the true boundary tests they are.

Each obstacle, though frustrating, offers a chance to strengthen your commitment to your new boundaries and realign with *Who You Are* and how you want to show up in the world. Just as you wouldn't bail on a road trip because your GPS took a wrong turn, you can use these challenges as reminders to pause, check your direction, and make any necessary changes to get back on track and keep moving toward your goals.

So, when challenges inevitably arise and shit goes sideways—celebrate!

It means you are moving beyond the limits of your comfort zone and are on the brink of a something truly transformative.

Does it feel awful? Definitely.

Is it normal? Absolutely.

Expanding Your Comfort Zone

This is all well and good, but let's be honest—no one likes it when life throws a curveball and messes up our carefully laid plans. Luckily, when things go ass-sideways and you're not sure what to do, you don't just have to grit your teeth and bear it.

In fact, you have a lot more power than you think.

While you might not realize it yet, you actually have a superpower. In every moment, you have the ability to choose how you want to respond to the challenges and setbacks that appear on your path. This ability to choose—to use your free will to move you toward your goals and desires —is your greatest gift and superpower. It allows you to decide how you want to react when life's GPS inevitably takes you down an unfamiliar road.

While many things in our world are beyond our control, how we respond to what is happening around us is always within our power. When you decide to compassionately hold a boundary with yourself, and make your own goals a priority, something incredible happens: your comfort zone expands to include the things you desire, making them feel more attainable and safer for your neurology.

Your decisions are what help shape the size of your comfort zone and they possess a powerful magic that can transform your life in immeasurable ways. This means, the more you continue to use the insights and tools you've gained on this journey, the more your comfort zone will expand, unlocking possibilities you've only dreamed of. And it all begins when you stop being 'Nice', start saying 'Yes' to yourself, and embrace a life guided by the wise presence of compassionate boundaries.

This is where your journey truly begins.

Welcome.

CHAPTER SEVENTEEN ACTIVITY
Putting It All Together

Now that you've figured out *Who You Are*, identified your core needs, learned how to share your desires, and practiced graciously receiving all the wonderful things that come your way, it's time to prepare for when life inevitably throws you curveballs.

This is your step-by-step guide for when life gets life-y and shit goes sideways.

Here, we'll bring everything together so you have a roadmap for handling those tough moments when emotions are running high and you're just holding on for dear life. Whether you're dealing with anxiety, overwhelm, anger, sadness, or any other intense feelings, this step-by-step guide will help you navigate through them more easily.

Step One: R.A.G.E.: Release Anger, Gain Empowerment

When emotions start boiling over and the tears won't stop falling, you need to give them an outlet that's not just bouncing around in your body or rattling around in your head. This is where the R.A.G.E. release really shines.

A reminder of how to R.A.G.E.: Start by physically releasing tension in your body. Punch a pillow, shake a washcloth, or try any other physical activity that helps you release pent-up energy. (Refer to Chapter 11 for a full list of ideas)

Next, write down anything you need to get out. Whether it's anger at yourself, frustration with the Universe, or irritation about anything else, pour it all out in your journal or notebook. Be raw and honest—no holding back.

Remember: You can't access your Core Essence when emotions are running the show so releasing pent-up emotional energy in this way frees up space for more mental clarity.

Step Two: Protect and Bubble your energy

After you have started to move the energy of your emotions through your body (they won't be gone, but they'll be in motion, which is better than letting them stagnate), it's time to help your neurology feel safe again. Remember that as humans, we tend to feel the safest when we can connect with the ground. Luckily, simply imagining this connection to the earth can be enough to convince our brains that we are okay.

Take a few deep breaths and imagine roots growing from the bottoms of your feet, anchoring deep into the Earth. Do this for 3-5 breaths. Then, check in on your Bubble—take a moment to notice it, whatever that means for you (seeing it, feeling it, hearing it, tasting it, or smelling it).

Feel free to refer back to Chapter 5 for a recap of how to build your energetic boundary.

Step Three: Access your need/desire

From a grounded state, where your nervous system feels safe, ask yourself, "Which of my Core Needs are not being met right now?" Refer to your list from the Chapter 9 activity and identify which unmet need(s) are causing the emotions you're feeling.

Step Four: Create a boundary

Once you have identified which of your Core Needs require more attention, it's time to establish a boundary to help meet them. Sometimes, this may involve setting a boundary with yourself around how you manage your time or prioritize self-care. Other times it will require you to speak up. This is where you can use the Boundaries Blueprint:

"I appreciate/I respect/I agree/I love (you)" + AND + "I would love..."

Quick Examples:

- I appreciate you want to spend time with me, and I would love a day to myself to recharge.

- I love you, and I would love more help around the house.
- I appreciate your perspective, and I would love my perspective to be considered as well.
- I respect your opinion, and I would love the freedom to express my quirks.

Step Five: Light up your soul

Speaking up and sharing your desires is an empowering process, but it does take energy. That's why it's important to replenish your energy before and after setting your boundaries. This is where doing something that truly Lights Up Your Soul becomes key. Refer back to your list from Chapter 8 and complete as many items as you can in whatever time you have available.

Remember: The only requirement is that you engage in an activity that brings a genuine smile to your face and joy to your heart, without needing assistance from others. While there are times when we need support from other people in our life, learning how to replenish our own energy is an essential skill we need to cultivate on our own.

Final Thoughts

When it comes to sharing authentic and truly compassionate boundaries, your job is to know what you desire, share it without conditions, and keep your energy full and ready to receive the goodness you asked for. While it may be tempting to skip over the awkward parts, following these steps, in this order, whenever faced with life's messiness, will help you move through it with more grace and ease, bringing you closer to the life you want—one boundary at a time.

WHEN SH*T GOES SIDEWAYS

CONCLUSION
Healing The World

"Regardless of what is going on in the world around you, your only job is to shine your light so bright you ignite the light in others."
- Jennifer Febel

As our time together draws to a close, I want to express my deepest gratitude to you for your willingness to embark on this transformative journey with me. In a world that often glorifies over-giving, over-achieving, and being 'Nice', it takes real courage to pursue a path dedicated to creating healthy boundaries and fostering authentic and compassionate connections.

Throughout our time together, we have explored a lot of new concepts to help you reclaim your power and live more authentically.

Here's a recap of the insights we've explored:

We learned how being overly 'Nice' can lead to burnout and a complete loss of self, and the importance of choosing to be compassionate instead.

We explored the impact of your inner narrative on your identity and took the first steps to beginning to rewrite your story.

CONCLUSION

We dug into the depths of *Who You Are* beyond societal labels and learned about the dynamics between your conscious and unconscious mind.

We examined how perception shapes your reality and how your past experiences influence present perceptions.

We explored the four layers of reality—physical, emotional, mental, and energetic—and how lacking boundaries can obscure your Core Essence.

We learned about your sphere of influence and the different energy flows within healthy boundary systems.

We discovered how to use the biggest jerks in your life as mirrors to help you identify and neutralize your own triggers.

We learned the difference between conditions and boundaries and how to ensure we avoid building walls.

We discovered the hidden wisdom and meaning of your emotions, and how to use them as powerful data and feedback.

We learned the *Boundaries Blueprint*, a simple and magical linguistic formula for sharing your boundaries and opening up a space for genuine connection.

We explored the art of compassionate negotiation and learned how to ask better questions to turn your boundary conversations into meaningful exchanges.

We learned the *Feedback Formula* and how to offer compassionate guidance to others as they learn to honor your boundaries.

We explored receptivity, the flipside of boundaries, and how it is fundamental to fostering healthy relationships.

We learned the science behind setbacks and how to move through them and build your resilience.

Most of all, we learned how to set healthy and effective boundaries without feeling like a gigantic dick.

HOW TO SET BOUNDARIES WITHOUT FEELING LIKE A D*CK

Shine Your Light So Bright

In Kabbalah, the mystical branch of Jewish tradition, there is a powerful concept called *Tikkun Olam*, which translates to "repair the world." This ancient teaching reminds us that each of us has a role in bringing balance and harmony to our world and teaches that within every individual lies a special inner light—a unique spark that connects us to others and to the energy around us. It is by recognizing and nurturing this light that we can make a profound impact and help illuminate the darkness.

Your purpose, therefore, is simple: to shine your light so bright that it ignites the light in others.

We all aspire to make a meaningful impact in the world and to leave each person we meet better than we found them. With the tools and wisdom you have gained here, you now have everything you need to be a catalyst for real change and inspiration in your life. By choosing to embrace healthy boundaries and offering compassion—without being '*Nice*'—you are setting the stage to create a life you thought you could only dream of.

Congratulations on all you have learned and accomplished here. May your path forward blossom more and more as you continue to step into the fullness of *Who You Are*. As you move forward on this new path, please know that if you need some additional support, I am just an email away and I would be honored to have you join me for one of my live or virtual events. And if you are looking for more personalized support, I offer that too.

Until we meet again, keep shining your light, honoring your boundaries with compassion and courage, and embracing the beautiful uniqueness of *Who You Are*.

Thank you for allowing me to be a part of your journey.

With gratitude,

Jen

Be Original. Own Boundaries. Shine.

CONCLUSION

About the Author

"You are not broken." This phrase has become Jennifer's personal and professional mantra and it is one she hopes to share with as many people as possible. After being diagnosed with over seven different mental health conditions by the age of 19, Jennifer embarked on a unique journey of healing and self-discovery that helped shape her belief that no one is broken and that healing is possible for anyone who seeks it out.

Today, as a board-designated Master Hypnotherapist, Emotional Resiliency Coach, Mentor, and Communications Instructor, Jennifer brings over 20 years of experience in psychology, communication, and linguistics to her work. Through her private practice, as well as her trainings and workshops, she empowers individuals to overcome their challenges by teaching them the same tools and principles that transformed her own life.

In her debut book, Jennifer invites readers to explore the space between their head and heart, learn to bridge the gap, and step into a version of themselves they never dreamed possible. Her approach blends professional insights with the wisdom gained from her own healing journey.

As someone who has walked this path herself, Jennifer understands firsthand how difficult it can be to navigate life's obstacles. Her mission is to help others find their own path to healing and wholeness by empowering them with the knowledge that they are never broken, only in need of understanding and growth.

Jennifer currently resides in Ontario, Canada, with her husband, Brian, her mother-in-law, Lee, and their fur family: Lexi, Stella, Colby, and Brie. She works with clients one-on-one and in groups, offering virtual sessions and training workshops to make support easy and accessible.

To learn more about upcoming retreats, courses and workshops, please visit: www.btgwellness.com. For those seeking deeper support and/or private sessions, please feel free to visit Jennifer's coaching website at: www.livelifeunbroken.com.

REFERENCES

References

[1] Emoto, Masaru. *The Hidden Messages In Water.* 2004.

[2] Perlman, Howard. *The Water in You.* December 2016.

[3] Freud, Sigmund. *The Interpretation of Dreams.* Translated by A. A. Brill, Macmillan, 1913. Originally published as *Die Traumdeutung* in 1899.

[4] Taylor, Jill Bolte. *My Stroke of Insight: A Brain Scientist's Personal Journey.* Viking, 2008.

[5] "Information Theory: Physiology." *Encyclopaedia Britannica*, accessed June 24, 2024, https://www.britannica.com/science/information-theory/Physiology.

[6] King, Serge Kahili. *Huna: Ancient Hawaiian Secrets for Modern Living.* Atria Books/Beyond Words, 2008.

[7] Jung, Carl. *The Archetypes and the Collective Unconscious.* Princeton University Press, 1968.

[8] Quantum Superposition. *Caltech Science Exchange*, accessed June 24, 2024, https://scienceexchange.caltech.edu/topics/quantum-science-explained/quantum-superposition.

[9] Choi, Charles Q. "The Double-Slit Experiment Gets Weirder Than Ever." *Popular Mechanics*, accessed June 24, 2024, https://www.popularmechanics.com/science/a22280/double-slit-experiment-even-weirder/.https://www.popularmechanics.com/science/a22280/double-slit-experiment-even-weirder/.

[10] Johnson, Robert A. *Inner Gold: Understanding Psychological Projection.* Paperback, July 26, 2017.

[11] HeartMath Institute. *Science of the Heart: Exploring the Role of the Heart in Human Performance.* 2018. HeartMath Institute,

REFERENCES

https://www.heartmath.org/research/science-of-the-heart/. Accessed August 2024.

[12] McCraty, R., Atkinson, M., Timofejeva, I., Joffe, R., Vainoras, A., Landauskas, M., & Alabdulgader, A. A. "The Influence of Heart Coherence on Synchronization Between Human Heart Rate Variability and Geomagnetic Activity." *Journal of Complexity in Health Sciences*, 1(2), 42-48. https://doi.org/10.21595/chs.2018.20480.

[13] Bowlby, J. *Attachment and Loss: Vol. 1. Attachment*. Basic Books, 1969. Ainsworth, M. D. S., Blehar, M. C., Waters, E., & Wall, S. *Patterns of Attachment: A Psychological Study of the Strange Situation*. Lawrence Erlbaum Associates, 1978.

[14] Rutter, M., Kumsta, R., Schlotz, W., & Sonuga-Barke, E. "Early Adolescent Outcomes for Institutionally-Deprived and Non-Deprived Adoptees. I: Disinhibited Attachment." *Journal of Child Psychology and Psychiatry*, 53(1), 22-30, 2012.

[15] Sparavigna, A. C., & Baldi, M. "A Mathematical Study of a Symbol: The Vesica Piscis of Sacred Geometry." *Philica*, January 2016. Retrieved from Philica.

[16] *The Devil Wears Prada*. Directed by David Frankel, performances by Meryl Streep and Anne Hathaway, 20th Century Fox, 2006.

[17] *Grease*. Directed by Randal Kleiser, performances by John Travolta and Olivia Newton-John, Paramount Pictures, 1978.

[18] Luskin, Frederic. *Forgive for Good: A Proven Prescription for Health and Happiness*. HarperOne, 2003.

[19] Sapolsky, Robert M. *Why Zebras Don't Get Ulcers: The Acclaimed Guide to Stress, Stress-Related Diseases, and Coping* (3rd ed.). Holt Paperbacks, 2004.

[20] *Animaniacs*. Directed by Dave McCurdy, produced by Tom Ruggeri and Rusty Mills, Warner Bros. Animation, 1993. "Yakko's World."

[21] *Wicked*. Directed by Joe Mantello, music and lyrics by Stephen Schwartz, performances by Idina Menzel and Kristin Chenoweth, Universal Stage Productions, 2003.

[22] Burch, Noel, and Gordon, Thomas. *Teacher Effectiveness Training*. Gordon Training International, 1974.

[23] Blanchard, K. H., & Johnson, S. *The One Minute Manager*. William Morrow, 1982.

[24] Zak, P. J., Stanton, A. A., & Ahmadi, S. "Oxytocin Increases Generosity in Humans." *PLoS ONE*, 2(11), e1128, 2007.

[25] Gottman, J. M., & Silver, N. (1999). *The Seven Principles for Making Marriage Work*. New York: Harmony Books.

[26] Yin, H. H., & Knowlton, B. J. "The Role of the Basal Ganglia in Habit Formation." *Nature Reviews Neuroscience*, 7(6), 464-476, 2006.

[27] Duhigg, Charles. *The Power of Habit: Why We Do What We Do in Life and Business*. Random House, 2012.

REFERENCES

Thank you for buying my book

If you are ready for even deeper growth, I would love to support you on your journey. Sign up for my newsletter at www.btgwellness.com to receive special offers, bonus content, and updates on my latest courses, trainings, and retreats.

To learn more about my private coaching sessions, please visit www.livelifeunbroken.com.

If you enjoyed this book, I would be so grateful if you could take a moment to leave a review on Amazon or Goodreads. Your feedback helps other readers discover the book and makes a huge difference for self-published authors like me.

Thank you for your support!

REFERENCES

www.ingramcontent.com/pod-product-compliance
Lightning Source LLC
Chambersburg PA
CBHW071233070526
44583CB00017B/2155